The ultimate Oslo travel gu

Wanderlust travel series

Your comprehensive travel Companion to Norway's vibrant

capital

John Walker

Disclaimer

Although the publisher and the author have made every effort to ensure that the information in this book was correct at press time, changes may be made over time therefore the author does not guarantee that the information herein is valid at all times.

While this publication is designed to provide accurate information regarding the subject matter covered, the publisher and the author assume no responsibility for errors, inaccuracies, omissions, or any other inconsistencies herein and hereby disclaim any liability to any party for any loss, damage, or disruption caused by errors or omissions, whether such errors or omissions result from negligence, accident, or any other cause.

This publication is meant as a source of valuable information for the reader, however, it is not meant as a substitute for direct expert assistance. If such a level of assistance is required, the services of a competent professional should be sought.

It is not recommended to use this book as a resource for legal, commercial, financial, or accounting guidance. We strongly suggest all readers consult with qualified experts in the disciplines of law, business, accounting, and finance.

Table of content

CHAPTER 1:

Introduction to oslo

Overview

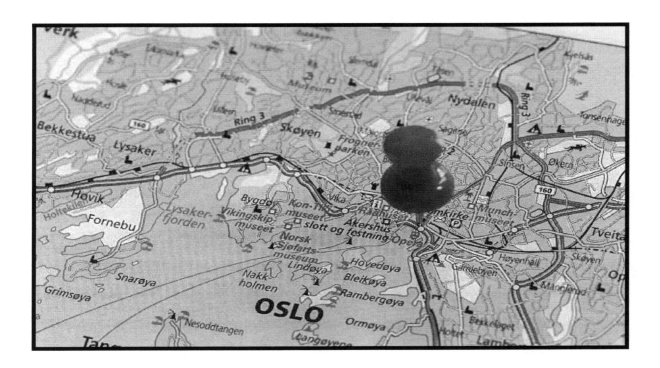

Oslo, the capital city of Norway, is a lively and cosmopolitan metropolis renowned for its breathtaking natural beauty, rich historical background, and exceptional quality of life. Positioned on the southern coast of the country, Oslo occupies a picturesque location between the Oslofjord and forested hills, seamlessly blending urban sophistication with the tranquility of nature.

With a population exceeding 670,000 residents and a greater metropolitan area surpassing one million people, Oslo stands as Norway's most populous city. It serves as the economic, political, and cultural heart of the nation, hosting the Norwegian government, royal family, and numerous international organizations.

Oslo possesses a captivating history spanning over a thousand years. Founded in the 11th century from its origins as a medieval trading hub to a fortified stronghold, Oslo has evolved into a modern and progressive city while preserving its historical landmarks.

One of Oslo's defining features is its strong connection to nature. Surrounded by forests, parks, and waterways, the city offers abundant opportunities for outdoor activities like hiking, skiing, and sailing. This proximity to nature is complemented by a commitment to sustainability, with Oslo recognized as one of the world's greenest cities, striving for carbon neutrality and promoting eco-friendly initiatives.

Culturally, Oslo embraces its artistic side with a thriving arts and music scene. The city is home to numerous museums, galleries, and performance venues, including the renowned Oslo Opera House and the Munch Museum, which showcases the iconic works of Norwegian artist Edvard Munch, including his famous piece, "The Scream."

The people of Oslo are known for their welcoming and inclusive nature, reflecting Norway's overall reputation for social equality and welfare. The city consistently ranks high in global quality of life indexes, thanks to its excellent education and healthcare systems, efficient public transportation, and emphasis on achieving a healthy work-life balance.

Oslo's culinary scene offers a diverse array of gastronomic delights, with a strong emphasis on fresh, locally sourced ingredients. Visitors can indulge in traditional Norwegian dishes such as salmon, cod, and reindeer, while also exploring international cuisines found in the city's multicultural neighborhoods.

Despite the cold and dark winters, the warm hospitality of Norwegians and the cozy cafes in this peaceful town will leave you longing for more. Summers are delightful, with bustling sidewalk cafes and parks filled with sun-seeking locals. Whether observing the boats at the pier or immersing oneself in the various museums, Oslo creates lasting memories for the future. While Oslo embodies the atmosphere of a small town, it also exudes the vibrancy of a big city. Exploring attractions like Vigeland's statue park, Munch's Museum, and the Folk Museum at Bygdoy provides a genuine glimpse into Norwegian life, both past and present. However, to fully appreciate the natural beauty of the surrounding areas and savor the extraordinarily long summer days, one must venture into the hills and deep forests.

History of Oslo

The earliest known settlement in the Oslo area dates back to around 1000 BCE when the region was inhabited by Norse tribes. However, it was during the Viking Age (800-1050 CE) that Oslo, then known as "Ánslo," emerged as an important trading hub. The Vikings used the Oslo Fjord as a strategic maritime route, allowing them to trade goods and raid neighboring lands.

In the early 11th century, King Harald Hardrada, one of Norway's most famous Viking kings, established Oslo as his capital. He constructed a fortification called Gamlebyen (Old Town) and made significant efforts to develop the city. However, Oslo's growth was hindered by frequent fires and political instability during the following centuries.

In the 14th century, Norway entered into a union with Denmark, and Oslo's importance declined as the capital was moved to Copenhagen. The city suffered from several devastating fires and the Black Death plague, which significantly reduced its population.

In the early 17th century, King Christian IV of Denmark-Norway decided to rebuild Oslo and renamed it Christiania after himself. The city was redesigned in a grid pattern, with wide streets and spacious squares. Christiania became the center of trade and administration in Norway, and its population steadily grew.

Norway gained independence from Denmark in 1814, and Christiania remained the capital. The city experienced rapid industrialization and urbanization in the 19th century, driven by the timber and shipping industries. Notable landmarks, such as the Royal Palace and the University of Oslo, were built during this time, reflecting the city's growing importance.

In 1925, Christiania officially renamed Oslo, reviving the historical name. The 20th century brought both prosperity and challenges to the city. During World War II, Oslo was occupied by Nazi Germany, enduring five years of occupation. After the war, Oslo played a vital role in the post-war reconstruction of Norway.

In recent decades, Oslo has become renowned for its commitment to environmental sustainability and urban planning. The city has implemented innovative initiatives to reduce carbon emissions and promote public transportation and cycling. Oslo's efforts were recognized when it was awarded the European Green Capital title in 2019.

Today, Oslo is a cosmopolitan city known for its modern architecture, cultural attractions, and quality of life. It is home to numerous museums. The city's waterfront area, known as Aker Brygge, has been transformed into a vibrant district with restaurants, shops, and recreational spaces. Oslo continues to evolve and adapt, embracing its historical roots while looking toward the future. With its blend of natural beauty, cultural heritage, and progressive mindset, Oslo remains a captivating city that showcases the resilience and spirit of Norway.

Culture

Oslo is known for its rich cultural heritage and vibrant modern scene, reflecting its history, values, and the diverse backgrounds of its residents. One of the defining characteristics of Oslo's culture is its strong connection to nature. Situated by the Oslo Fjord and surrounded by forests and hills, the city embraces outdoor activities and promotes a sustainable lifestyle. The residents of Oslo often engage in hiking, skiing, and cycling, making use of the extensive network of trails and green spaces.

The city places a strong emphasis on renewable energy, green spaces, and sustainable urban development. Oslo's citizens actively engage in eco-friendly practices, such as cycling, using public transportation, and recycling.

The city's dedication to sustainability extends to its architecture, with several notable environmentally conscious buildings, including the Powerhouse Brattørkaia, which produces more energy than it consumes. Oslo's focus on sustainability has not only earned it international acclaim but also influenced its cultural identity, with an increasing number of eco-friendly initiatives and events taking place throughout the city.

This harmonious relationship with nature permeates through the cultural activities and events in Oslo.

Art and design play a significant role in Oslo's cultural landscape. Furthermore, Oslo hosts a vibrant music scene, catering to a wide range of tastes and genres. The city also boasts numerous music festivals throughout the year, including the Øya Festival, and the Oslo Jazz Festival, which celebrates jazz in various venues across the city. From classical orchestras to underground bands, Oslo offers a diverse and dynamic music scene that appeals to different audiences.

The cuisine is another integral part of Oslo's culture. Norwegian cuisine reflects the country's connection to the sea and the abundance of natural resources. Oslo's restaurants and cafes offer a blend of traditional and innovative dishes, often featuring local ingredients such as seafood, game meat, and berries. Smoked salmon, cured meats, and traditional potato dishes like "lutefisk" and "rømmegrøt" are popular choices. The city also embraces international flavors, with a variety of global cuisines available to cater to its multicultural population. Food markets like Mathallen Oslo provide a platform for local producers and artisans to showcase their products, adding to the culinary diversity of the city.

In addition to the arts and gastronomy. The Nobel Peace Prize Ceremony held annually at Oslo City Hall is a globally recognized event that honors individuals and organizations making significant contributions to peace. Other notable festivals include the Oslo Pride Parade. Oslo culture also emphasizes education, innovation, and social welfare. Norway's strong commitment to education is reflected in the presence of prestigious academic institutions, including the University of Oslo, which is known for its research and academic excellence. Oslo's focus on innovation and sustainability is evident in its development of smart city solutions, renewable energy projects, and a thriving startup scene.

Weather and best time to visit

Oslo experiences a temperate oceanic climate with cool summers and mild winters. The best time to visit Oslo largely depends on your preferences and the activities you wish to engage in.

Overview of the weather and the recommended times to visit:

1. Summer (June to August):
   - Weather: Oslo's summers are pleasantly mild with average temperatures ranging from 15°C to 25°C (59°F to 77°F). The city experiences long daylight hours, and occasional rain showers are possible.
   - Summer is an ideal time to visit Oslo if you want to explore the city's outdoor attractions, such as Vigeland Park, Oslo Fjord, and

the Oslo Opera House. Additionally, this period coincides with many cultural festivals and events.

2. Spring (April to May) and Autumn (September to October):

- Weather: Spring and autumn in Oslo are characterized by mild temperatures, ranging from 5°C to 15°C (41°F to 59°F). The weather can be unpredictable, with alternating sunny and rainy days.
- Spring and autumn are excellent times to visit Oslo for those who prefer milder weather and fewer crowds. It's a great time to explore museums, visit historical sites, and enjoy the city's vibrant café culture.

3. Winter (November to March):

- Weather: Oslo's winters are cold, with temperatures ranging from -6°C to 3°C (21°F to 37°F). Snowfall is common, and daylight hours are shorter, especially in December.
- Winter is recommended for visitors who enjoy winter sports and activities, such as skiing, ice skating, and exploring the Christmas markets. The city offers a magical atmosphere during the holiday season.

Language in oslo

The primary language spoken in Oslo is Norwegian, which has two official written forms: Bokmål and Nynorsk. Bokmål is the more commonly spoken and used form in government documents and the media. English is also widely spoken and understood in Oslo, with many establishments and service providers offering English language support. However, learning some basic Norwegian can be beneficial for gaining a deeper understanding of Norwegian culture and history.

In addition to Norwegian and English, other languages spoken in Oslo include Sami (spoken by indigenous people of northern Scandinavia), Swedish (a neighboring language), Turkish, and Arabic (spoken by immigrant communities in Oslo).

A list of the Norwegian phrases you can use during your trip to Oslo:

1. Hello: Hei (pronounced "hey")

2. Goodbye: Hade (pronounced "hah-duh")

3. Please: Vennligst (pronounced "vehn-lihk-st")

4. Thank you: Takk (pronounced "tahk")

5. You're welcome: Bare hyggelig (pronounced "bah-ree hee-yuh-lihk")

6. Do you speak English?: Snakker du engelsk? (pronounced "snah-ker doo eng-lihk")

7. I don't speak Norwegian: Jeg snakker ikke norsk (pronounced "yehg snah-ker nee-koh norsh")

8. How are you?: Hvordan går det? (pronounced "hoo-dahn gah-der deh")

9. I'm fine, thank you: Jeg har det bra, takk (pronounced "yehg hahr deh brah, tahk")

10. Excuse me: Unnskyld meg (pronounced "oon-shulsh may")

11. Where is the bathroom?: Hvor er toalettet? (pronounced "vohr air toh-ah-let-teh")

12. Do you have any recommendations for restaurants?: Har du noen anbefalinger for restauranter? (pronounced "hah doo noh-en ahn-beh-ling-er for res-toh-rahn-ter")

13. How much does this cost?: Hvor mye koster dette? (pronounced "vohr mee koh-ster deh-steh")

14. I would like to buy this: Jeg vil gjerne kjøpe dette (pronounced "yehg vil jeh-neh kyuh-peh deh-steh")

15. Can you help me?: Kan du hjelpe meg? (pronounced "kahn doo yuh-hel-peh may")

16. I'm lost: Jeg er fortapt (pronounced "yehg air for-tahpt")

17. Can you call a taxi for me?: Kan du ringe en taxi til meg? (pronounced "kahn doo rihn-geh en tahk-see til may")

18. Sorry, I don't understand: Beklager, jeg forstår ikke (pronounced "beh-kah-lahr, yehg for-stah ih-kah")

19. Can you speak slower please?: Kan du snakke saktere, vær så snill? (pronounced "kahn doo snah-keh skah-teh-reh, vehr så snihl")

20. Do you have this in English?: Har du dette på engelsk? (pronounced "hah doo deh-steh pah eng-lihk")

21. I'm looking for the train station: Jeg ser etter togstasjonen (pronounced "yehg ser eh-ter toh-gah-sta-syehn")

22. I'm going to the museum: Jeg skal til museet (pronounced "yehg skal til moo-seh-eht")

23. I'm hungry: Jeg er sulten (pronounced "yehg air sul-ten")

24. I'm thirsty: Jeg er tørst (pronounced "yehg air thorst")

25. I need a doctor: Jeg trenger en lege (pronounced "yehg tren-ger en leh-geh")

26. Can you call the police?: Kan du ringe politiet? (pronounced "kahn doo rihn-geh po-li-see-ehn")

27. I'm tired: Jeg er sliten (pronounced "yehg air sli-ten")

28. I'm cold: Jeg er kald (pronounced "yehg air kahl")

29. I'm hot: Jeg er varm (pronounced "yehg air varm")

30. I'm lost: Jeg er fortapt (pronounced "yehg air for-tahpt")

31. I need help: Jeg trenger hjelp (pronounced "yehg tren-ger hjelp")

32. I'm allergic to (something): Jeg er allergisk mot (something) (pronounced "yehg air ahl-er-gisk moht (something)")

33. I have a disability: Jeg har en funksjonshemming (pronounced "yehg hah en funk-syohn-shehm-ming")

34. I don't feel well: Jeg føler meg ikke bra (pronounced "yehg foo-ler may nee-koh brah")

35. I'm pregnant: Jeg er gravid (pronounced "yehg air grah-vihd")

Currency

The official currency in Oslo is the Norwegian krone (NOK), represented by the symbol "kr."

Subdivisions:

The krone is divided into smaller units called øre. 100 øre make up 1 krone, although the use of øre coins has become less common in recent years.

Exchange Rate:

The Norwegian krone has a floating exchange rate, but it is also pegged to the euro. The fixed exchange rate is 1 NOK = 0.096 EUR. However, the exchange rate between the krone and other currencies may fluctuate.

Strength and Safe Haven Currency:

The Norwegian krone is generally considered a strong currency. During periods of economic uncertainty, it is often viewed as a safe haven currency, attracting investors seeking stability.

Handling currency

1. Preparing Currency: It is advisable to exchange some of your currency for Norwegian kroner before arriving in Oslo. This can be done at banks or currency exchange bureaus, and it may provide you with a more favorable exchange rate compared to exchanging money upon arrival.

2. Card Payments: Credit cards and debit cards are widely accepted in shops and restaurants throughout Oslo. It is convenient to rely on card payments for most transactions. However, it is still useful to have some cash on hand, particularly for smaller shops or establishments that may not accept cards or for situations where cash is preferred (e.g., using public transportation).

3. Exchange Rates: Since exchange rates can vary, it is recommended to check the current exchange rate before exchanging your currency. This will give you an idea of the value you can expect for your money.

By being aware of these currency-related details, you can better navigate financial transactions during your time in Oslo.

CHAPTER 2:

<u>Getting to oslo</u>

By Air

To get to Oslo by air, you have several options depending on your location and the availability of flights. General steps to help you plan your journey:

1. Find your nearest international airport: Determine which airport is closest to your current location or the most convenient for you to depart from. Consider both local and international airports.

2. Search for flights: Use flight search engines or websites to find flights to Oslo. Popular flight search engines include Google Flights, Skyscanner, and Kayak, or directly check with airlines that operate in your region. Enter your departure airport and Oslo (Oslo Airport, Gardermoen - OSL) as your destination. Specify your preferred travel dates and select the number of passengers.

3. Compare prices and airlines: Review the search results to compare prices, flight durations, layovers, and airlines. Choose the flight that best fits your preferences and budget.

4. Book your flight: Once you've selected a suitable flight, follow the prompts to book your tickets. Provide the necessary passenger information and make the payment as required.

5. Prepare travel documents: Ensure you have a valid passport that will remain valid for the duration of your trip. Check if you require a visa to enter Norway, depending on your nationality. Additionally, make sure you have any necessary supporting documents, such as travel insurance, if required.

6. Pack your bags: Prepare your luggage according to the airline's baggage policies and any relevant restrictions. Consider the weather and activities you plan to engage in during your stay in Oslo.

7. Arrive at the airport: On the day of your departure, arrive at the airport in advance to allow time for check-in, security procedures, and potential delays. Follow the instructions provided by your airline regarding baggage drop-off, check-in counters, and boarding gates.

8. Fly to Oslo: Board your flight and enjoy the journey to Oslo. The duration will vary depending on your departure location and any layovers.

9. Arrive at Oslo Airport, Gardermoen: Upon arrival at Oslo Airport, follow the signs for immigration and passport control, if applicable. Retrieve your checked baggage and proceed through customs.

10. Transportation from the airport to Oslo city center: From Oslo Airport, you have several options to reach the city center. The Airport Express Train (Flytoget) is a convenient and fast option, taking around 20 minutes. There are also local trains, buses, and taxis available. Choose the mode of transportation that suits your preferences and budget.

- International Flights: If you are traveling from outside of Norway, you can check for direct international flights to Oslo Gardermoen Airport (OSL), also known as Oslo Airport. Many major airlines offer direct flights to Oslo from various international destinations.

- Connecting Flights: If there are no direct flights available from your location, you might need to take a connecting flight through a hub city. Some common hub cities for flights to Oslo include Amsterdam, Frankfurt, Copenhagen, London, and Stockholm. You can check with airlines for connecting flight options to Oslo.

By train

To get to Oslo by train, you have several options depending on your starting location.

1. Research your route: Determine the train routes available from your departure location to Oslo. Use the most convenient route and

schedule for your trip. Consider factors such as travel time, connections, and cost. Websites like RailEurope (raileurope.com) or national railway websites are useful resources for finding train schedules and prices. Check the websites of national railway companies or use online travel platforms to find the most suitable options.

2. Choose your starting point: If you are already in Europe, you can easily reach Oslo by train from various cities. For instance, you might consider starting your journey from major European capitals such as Copenhagen, Stockholm, Berlin, or Amsterdam, as they often have direct train connections to Oslo.

- Stockholm, Sweden: There are direct train connections between Stockholm and Oslo. You can take a train from Stockholm Central Station (Stockholms Central Station) to Oslo Central Station (Oslo Sentralstasjon). The journey takes around 5-6 hours, and there are several departures throughout the day.

- Gothenburg, Sweden: From Gothenburg, you can take a train to Oslo. There are direct trains available, and the journey typically takes around 3-4 hours. Trains depart from Gothenburg Central Station (Göteborg Centralstation) and arrive at Oslo Central Station.

- Copenhagen, Denmark: To reach Oslo from Copenhagen, you'll need to take a combination of train and ferry. First, take a train from Copenhagen Central Station (København H) to Helsingør

Station. From Helsingør, walk to the nearby ferry terminal and board the ferry to Helsingborg, Sweden. After arriving in Helsingborg, take a train to Oslo. The total travel time is approximately 8-9 hours.

- Helsinki, Finland: Unfortunately, there are no direct train connections between Helsinki and Oslo. However, you can take a train from Helsinki to Stockholm and then proceed from Stockholm to Oslo as mentioned in the first option.

Websites like SJ (Swedish Railways) and NSB (Norwegian State Railways) provide information on train schedules, prices, and ticket reservations.

3. Purchase tickets: Depending on the train service and country, you may be able to buy your train tickets online in advance. Visit the official website of the respective national railway company or use trusted online platforms to book your tickets. Make sure to choose the correct departure and arrival stations.

4. Prepare for transfers: If your journey involves transfers, pay attention to the duration of layovers between trains. Ensure you have enough time to comfortably change trains and account for any potential delays. Familiarize yourself with the station layouts to make your transfers easier.

5. Arriving in Oslo: Once you arrive in Oslo, you will most likely disembark at Oslo Central Station (Oslo S). This centrally located

station is well-connected to local public transportation, making it convenient to reach your final destination within the city.

It's always good to have a backup plan in case of unexpected changes or disruptions to train services.

Car

1. Route Planning: Determine the best route to Oslo based on your starting location. Consider using GPS or online mapping services to find the most efficient and scenic route. Plan rest stops, fuel stations, and accommodation if needed along the way.

Road Conditions and Weather: Stay updated on the road conditions and weather forecasts during your journey. Norway can experience changing weather conditions, especially during the winter months, so be prepared for potential snow, ice, or rain. Adjust your driving accordingly and stay safe.

2. Documents and requirements. Ensure you have all the necessary documentation for your trip, such as a valid driver's license, vehicle registration, and proof of insurance. If you're traveling from another country, check if an International Driving Permit (IDP) is required.

3. Road Conditions: Check the road conditions before your departure. In Norway, roads are generally well-maintained, but weather

conditions can impact driving, especially in winter. Stay updated on any road closures, construction zones, or traffic advisories.

4. Tolls: Be aware that Norway has several toll roads, especially around urban areas. Some tolls are automatic and require a toll tag or electronic payment. Make sure you have the necessary equipment or information to pay tolls along your route.

5. Fuel: Fill up your tank before leaving and keep an eye on fuel stations along the way, especially if you're traveling long distances between cities. Prices may vary, so consider refueling in larger towns instead of remote areas where fuel might be more expensive.

6. Speed Limits and Traffic Rules: Familiarize yourself with the speed limits and traffic regulations in Norway. In urban areas, the speed limit is generally 50 km/h, while on highways, it can vary from 80 km/h to 110 km/h. Always adhere to the posted limits and follow traffic rules to ensure your safety.

7. Parking: If you plan to explore Oslo by car, check for parking options in advance. There are public parking lots and garages available in the city, but be aware that parking fees may apply. Consider using Park & Ride facilities located on the outskirts of the city and utilizing public transportation for inner-city exploration.

8. Environmental Zones: Oslo has implemented environmental zones in certain areas to reduce pollution. Check if your vehicle meets the

requirements for these zones and avoid entering restricted areas if you don't have the necessary permits or exemptions.

9. Safety Equipment: Ensure your vehicle is equipped with necessary safety items, such as reflective vests, warning triangles, and a first aid kit. It's also advisable to have an emergency contact number or roadside assistance service available.

10. Enjoy the Journey: Driving to Oslo can be a scenic and enjoyable experience. Take breaks when needed, enjoy the beautiful Norwegian landscapes, and make the most of your trip.

By bus

Traveling to Oslo by bus can be a convenient and the most cost-effective way to reach the city.

1. Bus Companies: Several bus companies operate routes to Oslo from various cities in Europe. Some popular ones include FlixBus, Nettbuss, and Swebus. Check their websites or bus ticketing platforms for schedules, fares, and availability.

2. Departure Points: Buses to Oslo may depart from major cities and transportation hubs in neighboring countries. Depending on your location, you can find buses departing from cities like Stockholm, Copenhagen, Gothenburg, Berlin, Amsterdam, and others.

3. Duration: The duration of the bus journey to Oslo will depend on your starting point. The travel time can vary significantly based on the distance and the number of stops along the way. For example, a bus journey from Stockholm to Oslo usually takes around 7-9 hours.

4. Facilities: Most long-distance buses offer comfortable seating, air conditioning, onboard restrooms, and sometimes Wi-Fi connectivity. However, the amenities can vary between different bus operators and specific routes. Check the details provided by the bus company before booking.

5. Tickets and Booking: You can book your bus tickets online through the bus company's website or other third-party platforms. It's advisable to book your tickets in advance, especially during peak travel seasons, to secure your seat and potentially get better prices.

6. Border Crossings: If you're traveling from a different country to reach Oslo, make sure to check the visa requirements and any border crossing regulations that may apply. Verify if you need any specific travel documents.

7. Arrival in Oslo: Buses usually arrive at the Oslo Bus Terminal (Oslo Bussterminal) located in the city center. From there, you can easily access public transportation options like buses, trams, and the metro to reach your destination within Oslo.

By boat

Traveling by boat to Oslo can be a scenic and enjoyable experience. While Oslo is not directly accessible by boat from all locations, you can reach the city by taking a ferry or cruise ship to one of the nearby ports and then continuing your journey by land.

If you are traveling from international destinations, you may find cruise ships or ferries that offer routes to Oslo or nearby ports in Norway. These routes can vary depending on the season and the cruise or ferry company you choose. Common embarkation points for cruises to Oslo include Copenhagen, Denmark, and Kiel, Germany. It's advisable to check with various cruise operators or ferry companies to see if they offer routes to Oslo from your location. There are various modes of water transportation available, including cruise ships, ferries, private yachts, and boats.

Cruise Ship: One option is to take a cruise ship that includes Oslo as a port of call. Many cruise lines offer itineraries that include Oslo, allowing you to enjoy the journey and explore other destinations along the way. Cruise ships typically dock at the Port of Oslo, which is conveniently located near the city center.

Ferry: Another option is to take a ferry from various destinations such as Denmark or Germany. Companies like Color Line, DFDS Seaways, and Stena Line operate ferry services to Oslo. These ferries offer overnight cabins, restaurants, entertainment, and other amenities to make your journey comfortable.

Private Yacht or Sailboat: If you have your own yacht or sailboat, you can sail to Oslo and dock at one of the marinas or guest harbors available.

Coastal Express: Hurtigruten, a famous Norwegian coastal express, operates ships that sail along the stunning Norwegian coastline. While the main route goes from Bergen to Kirkenes, you can embark or disembark at various ports, including Oslo. This option allows you to experience the beauty of the Norwegian coast before reaching Oslo.

Once you reach a nearby port, you can easily travel to Oslo by train or bus. For example, if you arrive in Copenhagen, you can take a train from Copenhagen Central Station to Oslo Central Station. The train journey offers beautiful views of the Scandinavian countryside.

Alternatively, if you prefer a more leisurely and scenic route, you can take a ferry from Copenhagen to Oslo. Several ferry companies operate this route, and the journey typically takes around 16-18 hours. The ferries are well-equipped with amenities, including cabins, restaurants, and entertainment options, ensuring a comfortable voyage.

When planning your trip, it's essential to check the schedules, availability, and pricing of various cruise lines, ferries, trains, or buses. Additionally, consider the time of year, as some routes may have limited availability during certain seasons.

CHAPTER 3:

Leverage on oslo pass

With the Oslo Pass you save both time and money while exploring the wonderful city.

Purchase and activation

You can buy the pass in advance, and activate it when you arrive in Oslo. Purchasing the Oslo Pass can be done through two options. The first option is to acquire it through the Oslo Pass app, where you can conveniently purchase the pass before your visit to Oslo and activate it upon arrival. The app, called "Oslo Pass – Official City Card," is accessible for both iPhone and Android users.

Alternatively, you have the option to purchase the Oslo Pass within Oslo itself. Numerous locations in the city offer the pass for sale, such as the Oslo Visitor Centre, Ruter's customer center, various accommodations, and select museums. However, please be aware that certain outlets may only sell Oslo Passes during the summer season, and the availability of different pass types may vary. It is advisable to directly contact the outlets to confirm their opening hours and the specific Oslo Pass types they offer. Additionally, it is important to note that the Oslo Pass with a student discount can only be purchased at the Oslo Visitor Centre and Ruter's customer center.

You can therefore wait to activate it until the first time you are going to use it, for example when you are going to take a bus or enter a museum. A countdown will then start from 24/48/72 hours, so you can always see how long it is until the pass expires.

Mobile version

You can buy an Oslo Pass for 24, 48 or 72 hours, for children, adults and seniors. You can buy several passes on the same phone. Please note that Oslo Pass users must then travel and visit the attractions together. It is possible to buy several passes on the same device for use on different days, but be careful not to activate them all at the same time. It is also not possible to transfer the Oslo Pass between devices.

Offline use

You must be online when purchasing the pass, but it can be used without an internet connection.

Note: The phone must be online when you activate the pass, as well as once every morning before using the pass so that the control code for the transport ticket is updated.

Validation

Before entering an attraction or traveling by public transport, make sure that your Oslo Pass is activated in the app. You must be online to activate the pass. The pass will then start a countdown for the time the pass is valid: 24, 48 or 72 hours.

Paper version

Validation

Before using the Oslo paper Pass, it is necessary to validate it by filling in the date, month, year, and time in the designated fields using a ballpoint pen. Once validated, the pass remains valid for the specified number of hours: 24, 48, or 72.

Usage on public transportation

When using public transportation, ensure that you have validated your pass prior to boarding. You only need to present your pass if there is a ticket inspection or to the bus driver if you enter through the front.

Spend on attractions

At museums and attractions, you must show your validated Oslo Pass at the ticket office. Click on "QR code" to bring up the QR code. The staff will scan the code before you enter. Note that you can only use the pass once per day at one and the same attraction.

Language

Information and explanations in the app are in English.

Price/payment

It costs nothing to download the app itself, you only pay when you buy an Oslo Pass.

There is a discounted price for children (under 18) and seniors (67 and older).

You pay with Visa/Master Card in the app by entering your card details.

Note that it is not possible to buy an Oslo Pass with a student discount in the app.

FAQ and Important points to consider:

- Is transportation to the airport covered by the Oslo Pass?

No, transportation to Oslo Airport (OSL) and Sandefjord Airport Torp is not included in the Oslo Pass. These airports are located outside zone 2.

- Does the Oslo Pass include the public ferry to Drøbak?

  No, the Oslo Pass does not cover the ferry to Drøbak as it travels through zones 3 and 4. However, the public bus to Drøbak is included.

- Are the Hop On-Hop Off buses and boats included in the Oslo Pass?

  No, the Hop On-Hop Off buses and boats are not included in the Oslo Pass.

- Can I switch between a physical card and a digital card?

  No, it is not possible to convert your physical card into a digital card or vice versa.

Terms of use

The Oslo Pass will not be refunded or replaced if it remains unused, activated, lost, or stolen. The mobile pass will also not be refunded if the app is uninstalled with unused or validated passes, or if the phone is damaged.

To use the Oslo Pass, you must validate it the first time you use it. This involves writing the date, year, and time on the card with a ballpoint pen in the designated field. If you validate the pass at the first museum you visit, the QR code on the back will be scanned, and that time will be considered the activation time. For the mobile pass, you need to activate it in the app by clicking on "Activate" the first time you use it.

When using public transport, ensure that the Oslo Pass is valid for the entire journey. If you are found traveling with an invalid or expired pass during a ticket inspection, you may be fined up to NOK 1,150. Additional information about public transport in Oslo and Akershus and ticket control fees can be found at ruter.no.

The Oslo Pass for children is valid for those aged 6 to 17, while the Oslo Pass senior is applicable to individuals aged 67 and older. Keep in mind that different attractions and activities may have varying age limits for children's tickets, so it's important to check these limits before purchasing the Oslo Pass to determine your potential savings.

Students up to the age of 30 can avail a 20% discount on the Oslo Pass. However, note that student discounts are only offered at the Oslo Visitor Center and Ruter's customer center at Oslo S, and a valid student ID with a photo is required. The student discount is not available for the mobile version of the Oslo Pass.

The Oslo Pass can only be used once per day at the same attraction.

For further knowledge, you can contact the tourist information call center at (+47) 23 10 62 00, available from Monday to Friday between 09.00 and 16.00.

Discounts available with the Oslo Pass

The Oslo Pass offers various discounts on activities and attractions. You can enjoy a 15% discount on fjord sightseeing with Båtservice Sightseeing, a 20% discount at select restaurants, discounted tickets for outdoor activities, and discounted entrance tickets to Tusenfryd amusement park. Additionally, you can avail discounted tickets for concerts by the Oslo Philharmonic and for a tour of the Opera. There are many more offers included as well.

Places where you can save with the Oslo Pass:

- Skimore Oslo: The largest ski resort in the Oslo area with 18 runs catering to all skill levels.
- Oslo Philharmonic: One of Europe's top orchestras, offering regular concerts at the Oslo Concert Hall and touring both domestically and internationally.
- The Scotsman: A large pub and restaurant located in the heart of Karl Johan, featuring four different sections.
- Boat Service Sightseeing: Provides guided boat and bus trips in Oslo throughout the year, drawing on over 70 years of sightseeing experience on the Oslofjord.
- Tregaarden's Christmas House: A store offering a wide range of Christmas decorations and items.
- Rorbua: A restaurant specializing in authentic North Norwegian cuisine, offering a pleasant dining experience.

- TusenFryd: Norway's largest classic amusement park, with over 30 exciting attractions and special features for younger visitors.

- The Norwegian Opera & Ballet: Oslo's opera house, situated by the fjord and characterized by its unique architectural design.

- The Happy Pig: A gastropub serving honest Norwegian food and quality drinks for both lunch and dinner, with outdoor seating available.

- New Delhi Restaurant: A top-notch establishment offering modern Indian cuisine.

- Skimore Oslo - Summer Park: One of Scandinavia's largest and most beautiful climbing parks, conveniently located just 30 minutes from central Oslo.

- Jarmann Gastropub: A gastropub situated in industrial premises at Aker Brygge, providing a view of the Oslofjord and Akershus Fortress. The menu offers something for everyone.

- Oslo Climbing Park: An adventurous climbing park set in wild and picturesque surroundings, featuring eight exciting treetop climbing routes, Tarzan jumps, and ziplines.

- Kaffistova: A Norwegian restaurant renowned for its well-prepared traditional dishes, including rasp balls, meat cakes, and generous portions of steamed salmon.

- The Well: An oasis for relaxation and rejuvenation of both the body and soul, offering a respite from the demands of everyday life.

- The Viking Planet: Norway's first digital Viking museum, allowing visitors to explore the Viking Age through a multisensory experience.

- Listen to Baljit: A colorful and informal Indian street food eatery located in Frogner.

Free with the Oslo Pass

Places where you can gain free admission:

- Akershus Castle: Within the castle at Akershus fortress, you can discover the remnants of the original medieval castle and explore the rooms that once housed Danish-Norwegian kings.
- The Labor Museum: Located in Sagene, this museum sheds light on the intriguing and lesser-known history of life along the Akerselva River.
- Astrup Fearnley Museum: Situated on Tjuvholmen, this museum showcases international contemporary art in a stunning landmark.
- The City Museum: Through diverse exhibitions, this museum offers insights into Oslo's history. One notable exhibition is "OsLove," which presents the city's history.
- The International Children's Art Museum: Experience the world through the eyes of children in this museum.
- Ekebergparken Sculpture Park: Just a few minutes away from the city center by tram, Ekebergparken combines a rich history, picturesque nature, and impressive sculptures.
- The Defense Museum: Delve into Norwegian military history at the beautiful Akershus Fortress.

- Frammuseet: Step aboard Fram, the world's strongest wooden ship, which has ventured to the northernmost and southernmost points of the Earth.
- Frognerbadet: A popular outdoor pool, perfect for summer, featuring two 50-meter pools, a paddling pool, and a diving tower.
- Henie Onstad Art Centre: Located in Bærum, west of Oslo, this museum showcases modern and contemporary art and has been open since 1968.
- Historical Museum: Explore the largest collection of prehistoric and medieval artifacts found in Norway.
- The HL Centre: Situated in Villa Grande, Quisling's former residence on Bygdøy, this center focuses on the Holocaust and minorities.
- Holmenkollen Ski Museum & Jumping Tower: Enjoy the best panoramic view of Oslo from this iconic ski museum and jumping tower.
- Intercultural Museum: Shedding light on the history of immigration and cultural changes in Norwegian society, this museum offers varied exhibitions in its gallery.
- The Kon-Tiki Museum: Learn about Thor Heyerdahl's famous expedition across the Pacific in 1947 on the balsa raft Kon-Tiki.
- Artists' House: Immerse yourself in Norwegian and international contemporary art within traditional surroundings.
- MUNCH: Discover the artistry and life of Edvard Munch in a completely new and immersive way.
- The National Museum: Visit the largest art museum in the Nordic region, featuring both old and modern art.

- Natural History Museum: Explore the remarkable diversity of nature in the heart of the city.

- Nobel Peace Center (temporarily closed): This unique museum presents inspiring stories about the Nobel Peace Prize and people's efforts for peace.

- Nordic Bible Museum: Embark on an exciting journey through biblical history with over 5,500 Bibles.

- Norway's Home Front Museum: Gain insight into the most significant events that occurred in Norway during the German occupation at this museum within Akershus Fortress.

- Norwegian Folk Museum: Step back in time at one of the world's largest open-air museums.

- Norwegian Maritime Museum: Immerse yourself in captivating stories within a unique maritime environment.

- Oslo City Walks: Join guided walks in Norwegian and English on Saturdays, Sundays, and Mondays throughout the year. One example is the "In the Heart of Oslo" walk on Saturdays at 14:00.

- Oslo Reptile Park: See live snakes, monkeys, crocodiles.

CHAPTER 4:

Accommodation in oslo

When looking for accommodation options in Oslo, you'll find a variety of choices to suit different preferences and budgets. Here are some popular options:

1. Hotels: Oslo has a wide range of hotels, from luxurious 5-star properties to budget-friendly options. Some popular areas for hotels include the city center (Sentrum), Aker Brygge, and Grünerløkka.

2. Bed and Breakfasts (B&Bs): B&Bs offer a more intimate and cozy experience, often located in residential areas. They provide a comfortable stay with breakfast included. Check out areas like Majorstuen or Frogner for B&B options.

3. Apartments and Vacation Rentals: Renting an apartment or vacation rental can be a great option for families or travelers looking for a home-like experience. Websites such as Airbnb, Booking.com, and VRBO offer a wide range of options in different neighborhoods throughout the city.

4. Hostels: Oslo has several hostels that cater to budget-conscious travelers. They provide dormitory-style accommodation and often have communal areas where you can meet fellow travelers. Some popular hostels include Anker Hostel, Oslo Youth Hostel Haraldsheim, and Central City Hostel.

5. Guesthouses: Guesthouses are smaller accommodations that offer a more personal touch. They are usually family-run and provide a cozy atmosphere. Look for guesthouses in residential areas or outskirts of the city.

6. Camping: If you enjoy outdoor adventures, Oslo offers several camping options. You can find campsites in and around the city, providing access to nature while still being relatively close to urban amenities.

When choosing your accommodation, consider factors such as location, budget, amenities, and proximity to public transportation. It's also worth checking reviews and comparing prices to find the best option that suits your needs.

Workation

Experience a "workcation" in Oslo if you are a freelancer, a remote worker, or someone who wants to combine work and travel. Stay in one of the hotels listed below, which cater to the needs of business and leisure travelers.

- Thon Hotel Cecil: Located in the heart of Oslo city center, this hotel offers easy access to restaurants, nightlife, shopping, and attractions.
- Karl Johan Hotel: Situated in a central location on Karl Johans gate, this hotel provides convenient access to the city's main street.
- Radisson Blu Scandinavia Hotel: This large, full-service hotel is adjacent to Slottsparken and offers proximity to attractions, shopping, and public transport.
- Radisson Blu Plaza Hotel Oslo: As Norway's tallest hotel, it is centrally located near Oslo Central Station, with easy access to shopping, restaurants, and museums.
- Territory: A hotel and meeting point situated in the middle of the city center.
- Radisson Blu Hotel Nydalen: This innovative and modern hotel is located by Akerselva in Nydalen, just 11 minutes away from the center by subway.
- Thon Hotel Opera: A large hotel with great facilities and guest rooms that offer a splendid view of Bjørvika and the Opera.
- Frogner House Apartments: Experience Oslo like a local by staying in these apartments, which provide a homely atmosphere.
- Clarion Hotel Oslo: An exclusive business and art hotel located in Barcode.
- Thon Hotel Arena: Situated in Lillestrøm, this hotel is conveniently located near the train station and the Norwegian Trade Fair, just a short train ride away from Oslo.

Accommodation for nature lovers

If you're a nature lover, Oslo offers various accommodations that allow you to immerse yourself in the natural surroundings.

- Scandic Holmenkollen Park: This hotel is situated in a tranquil area 350 meters above Oslo, providing a stunning view of the city and the fjord. It is the oldest part of.

- Topcamp Bogstad Camping: Located on the outskirts of Oslo near Nordmarka, this campground is open year-round and offers a rural and scenic setting, perfect for outdoor enthusiasts.

- Thon Hotel Storo: A newly built hotel conveniently located between Storo and Nydalen, just a 10-15 minute subway ride from the city center. It is situated in close proximity to.

- Radisson Blu Hotel Nydalen: This modern hotel with 185 comfortable guest rooms is situated by the Akerselva river in Nydalen, a mere 11 minutes away from the city center by subway.

- Thon Hotel Linne: A contemporary conference hotel with 394 comfortable rooms, centrally located in the northern part of Oslo and offering easy access to.

- Oscarsborg Hotel & Resort: Stay close to the Oslofjord at this unique fortress hotel located on an island in the Drøbaksundet, approximately 35 kilometers south of Oslo.

- Voksenåsen Hotel: Perched atop Holmenkollen, this hotel boasts one of Oslo's best views from an elevation of 501 meters above sea level. Its exceptional location and historical significance.

- Light Bow: Another hotel situated at the top of Holmenkollen, offering 85 guest rooms, a restaurant, function rooms, and meeting facilities. It provides easy access to hiking trails, ski slopes, and alpine resorts.
- Thon Hotel Ullevaal Stadium: A modern conference hotel directly connected to Norway's national football arena, Ullevaal Stadium. The hotel is conveniently located just ten minutes away from.

Accommodations for Weekend trips

If you're planning a weekend trip, Oslo is an ideal destination! The city is compact, allowing you to explore and enjoy a variety of experiences without the need for extensive travel.

Here are some hotels in Oslo that are recommended for a weekend trip:

- Thon Hotel Cecil: Located in the heart of Oslo city center, this hotel offers easy access to restaurants, nightlife, shopping, and attractions.
- Karl Johan Hotel: A centrally located hotel on Karl Johans gate, offering convenience and proximity to popular sights.
- Thon Hotel Europe: A newly renovated city hotel in the center of Oslo, within walking distance to Karl Johans gate, the Castle, the National Gallery, and major attractions.

- K7 Hotel Oslo (Formerly Saga Hotel Oslo Central): Situated in the center of Oslo, this hotel offers various room types to accommodate different needs.
- Scandic Victoria: A hotel right in the heart of Oslo, within walking distance to Oslo City Hall, Karl Johans gate, Aker Brygge, shopping, and restaurants.
- Citybox Oslo: An economy hotel in the city center, offering simple rooms and affordable prices, just five minutes away from Oslo Central Station.
- Thon Hotel Opera: A large hotel with great amenities and guest rooms overlooking Bjørvika and the Opera House.
- Frogner House Apartments: Stay in an apartment in Oslo and experience the city like a local. Frogner House Apartments provide a home-like experience.
- Amerikalinjen: A boutique hotel located in Amerikalinjen's old headquarters at Jernbanetorget.
- Clarion Hotel The Hub: Norway's largest hotel with 810 guest rooms spread over 13 floors.
- Thon Hotel Terminus: A comfortable hotel in the city center, close to entertainment, food, drinks, and shopping.
- Hotel Continental: A five-star hotel and restaurant in the heart of Oslo, near the National Theatre and Aker Brygge.
- Thon Hotel Gyldenløve: Centrally located on Oslo's west side, in the popular shopping street of Bogstadveien, offering guest rooms in seven different sizes.
- Thon Hotel Spectrum: Conveniently located near the Bus Terminal, Oslo Central Station, Oslo Spektrum, and Oslo City.

- Grand Hotel: A deluxe, full-service business hotel on Oslo's famous main street, Karl Johan, close to shopping, cultural offerings, and attractions.

Accommodation for Families

If you're traveling with your family, finding the right accommodation is important. Different families have different needs, whether it's location, price, or ample space for everyone. Luckily, there are hotels and other options in Oslo that cater to families.

Apartment: Renting a separate apartment is an excellent choice for families who want plenty of space and a comfortable stay. Having a kitchen available can make you feel at home in Oslo.

- Frogner House Apartments: These apartments offer a local experience, allowing you to live like a resident in Oslo. They provide spacious and comfortable accommodations.
- Thon Hotel Slottsparken: This apartment hotel is centrally located on the west side of the city center, with the Castle as its nearest neighbor. It offers 253 rooms and is suitable for families.
- Thon Hotel Linne: This modern conference hotel is located in the north of Oslo, with easy access to the city center. It has 394 comfortable rooms, including family-friendly options.
- Territory: This hotel is located in the middle of the city center and serves as a meeting point for visitors.

If you prefer camps, you can consider the following option:

- Topcamp Bogstad Camping: Open all year round, this camping site is located in a rural and scenic area on the border with Nordmarka. It offers a chance to enjoy nature while being close to the city.

If you're specifically looking for family rooms in hotels, here are some options:

- Thon Hotel Astoria: A budget hotel located in the city center with various amenities nearby.
- Thon Hotel Cecil: Situated in the heart of Oslo, this hotel offers easy access to restaurants, nightlife, shopping, and attractions.
- Karl Johan Hotel: Centrally located on Karl Johans gate, this hotel provides convenient access to Oslo's main attractions.
- Scandic Holmenkollen Park: Located 350 meters above Oslo, this hotel offers great views of the city and the fjord.
- Scandic Helsfyr: A centrally located hotel in a quiet area.
- Coch's Pensionat: A traditional boarding house near Slottsparken with a central location and good standard.
- Radisson Blu Scandinavia Hotel: A large full-service hotel with attractions, shopping, and public transport in the immediate vicinity.
- Radisson Blu Plaza Hotel Oslo: Norway's tallest hotel, centrally located near Oslo Central Station.

- Thon Hotel Europe: A newly renovated city hotel within a short walking distance to major attractions.
- K7 Hotel Oslo (formerly Saga Hotel Oslo Central): Located in the center of Oslo with various room types to choose from.
- Radisson Blu Hotel Nydalen: An innovative and modern hotel by Akerselva in Nydalen, just 11 minutes from the center by subway.
- Scandic Victoria: A hotel in the heart of Oslo within walking distance to major landmarks.
- Citybox Oslo: An economy hotel in central Oslo with simple rooms and affordable prices.
- Clarion Hotel The Hub: Norway's largest hotel with numerous guest rooms.
- Anchor Hotel (Anker Hotel): An affordable and centrally located hotel, providing a comfortable base for exploring Oslo.
- Thon Hotel Terminus: A comfortable hotel in the city center, offering easy access to entertainment, food, shopping, and more.
- Thon Hotel Gyldenløve: Centrally located in west Oslo, this hotel is situated on the popular shopping street Bogstadveien.
- Thon Hotel Spectrum: This hotel is centrally located near the bus terminal, Oslo Central Station, and Oslo Spektrum.
- Saga Hotel Oslo: A cozy hotel in central Oslo west, a short walk from Bogstadveien.
- Hotel Bondeheimen: A traditional hotel in the center of Oslo with modern facilities, operating since 1913.
- Thon Hotel Oslo Airport: Located just ten minutes from Oslo Airport Gardermoen, this hotel is suitable for both stays and small gatherings.

Cheap accommodations in oslo

There are many affordable options for accommodation in Oslo, despite the common perception that everything in the city is expensive. Even the cheapest hotels in Oslo are typically rated at least 3 stars and often include breakfast and free Wi-Fi. Here are some low-cost accommodation options in Oslo:

- Anchor Hotel: An affordable and centrally located hotel, providing a comfortable base for exploring Oslo.
- Topcamp Bogstad Camping: Located on the outskirts of Oslo, this camping site offers a scenic and rural setting, just a short drive from the city.
- Hotel Bondeheimen: A traditional hotel in the city center, equipped with modern facilities. It has been welcoming guests since 1913.
- Coch's Pensionat: A traditional boarding house situated near Slottsparken (the Royal Palace Park), offering a combination of a central location, good standard, and a pleasant atmosphere.
- Thon Hotel Astoria: A budget hotel located in the city center, with easy access to restaurants, bars, shops, and attractions.
- Citybox Oslo: An economy hotel in central Oslo, featuring simple rooms and affordable prices. It's just a five-minute walk from Oslo Central Station, and free Wi-Fi is available.

- K7 Hotel Oslo (Formerly Saga Hotel Oslo Central): This accommodation option in the city center offers ten different room types to cater to various preferences and budgets.

Accommodation with spa and wellness

You can escape the hustle and bustle of everyday life and indulge in a relaxing experience at one of Oslo's spa hotels. Whether you're looking for a hotel that specializes in spa services or one with excellent spa facilities as part of their offerings, Oslo has options to suit your needs.

If your main focus is the spa experience, The Thief is the perfect choice for you. This exclusive and elegant design hotel on Tjuvholmen is dedicated to providing a pure spa experience, with 114 rooms and suites, each featuring a private balcony.

Alternatively, there are other hotels in central Oslo that may not specialize in spas but still offer excellent spa departments. These include the American Line, Clarion Hotel, The Hub, Grand Hotel, and Radisson Blu Plaza Hotel. These hotels provide the perfect opportunity for some relaxing breaks during your stay in the city.

For a nature-infused spa experience, Lysebu is located near Nordmarka and offers access to a wellness area. Here, you can enjoy ultimate relaxation in the pool, sauna, or with a massage from the hotel's masseur after a day of exploring the nearby forest.

Unique hotels

If you are intrigued by interior design and aesthetics, or you value the special experiences and gifts that come with traveling, Oslo offers a variety of boutique hotels and other distinctive accommodations that will ignite your senses and inspire your photography. Your vacation photos from these hotels are bound to impress your loved ones.

Furthermore, some of these hotels boast a more intimate and personalized atmosphere, with a smaller number of rooms compared to traditional hotels. If you seek a secluded location, they provide the perfect setting in the midst of serene surroundings.

- Camilla's Hus: This first-class boutique hotel offers seven unique guest rooms in a house from 1845. It's located in a pleasant area behind the Castle.
- Thon Hotel Rosenkrantz Oslo: This design hotel is centrally located in Oslo, within walking distance of Karl Johans gate, public transport, shopping, and major attractions.
- Saga Hotel Oslo: This cozy hotel is located in central Oslo west, just a few minutes' walk from Bogstadveien. The building has been newly restored and dates back to the 1890s.

For newer and trendy options:

- Clarion Hotel Oslo: An exclusive business and art hotel situated in the Barcode district. It combines modern design with luxurious amenities.
- Sommerro: A neighborhood house that offers a range of facilities and services for a luxurious stay in Oslo.
- Amerikalinjen: This boutique hotel is a new trendy hotel situated in Amerikalinjen's old headquarters at Jernbanetorget. It features a well-thought-out interior and an intimate atmosphere.

If you're looking for something more budget-friendly unique hotel, you can consider:

- Cochs Pensjonat: This historic hotel is located directly behind the Castle and offers rooms of different sizes and price ranges. Some rooms even have a mini kitchen.

For luxurious experience, you can consider:

- Grand Hotel: This deluxe, full-service business hotel is located in the middle of Oslo's famous main street, Karl Johan. It offers a luxurious experience and is close to shopping, cultural offerings, and sights.
- Hotel Continental: This five-star hotel and restaurant is located in the center of Oslo, close to the National Theater and Aker Brygge.

- Hotel Bristol: This hotel is rich in tradition and known for its elegant style. It puts quality first and offers a luxurious stay.
- THE THIEF

If you're interested in breathtaking views, you can consider:

- Radisson Blu Plaza Hotel Oslo: This hotel is centrally located by Oslo Central Station and offers the best view with its 37 floors. The Top Restaurant & Bar on the 34th floor provides Norway's highest dining experience.

CHAPTER 5:

<u>Oslo fjord</u>

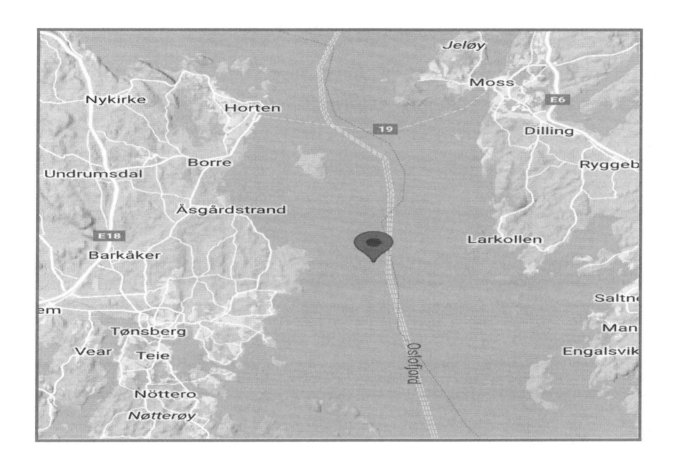

Oslo Fjord is a stunning natural feature located in Norway, just south of the city of Oslo. It stretches approximately 100 kilometers from the open sea into the heart of Oslo, offering breathtaking landscapes, islands, and a wide range of recreational activities. If you're planning a visit to Oslo Fjord.

Getting There

By Air: Fly to Oslo Airport (OSL), the largest international airport in Norway. From there, you can take a train or taxi to Oslo city center, where you can easily access the fjord.

By Train: If you're traveling within Europe, you can also reach Oslo by train and continue your journey to the fjord from there.

Exploring the Fjord

Museums: Take a trip to Bygdøy Peninsula, located on the western side of the fjord, which is home to several world-class museums. Visit the Viking Ship Museum to see remarkably preserved Viking ships, the Fram Museum to learn about polar exploration, and the Kon-Tiki Museum to explore Thor Heyerdahl's adventurous expeditions.

Boat Tours: One of the best ways to experience Oslo Fjord is by taking a boat tour. Several companies offer guided tours departing from Oslo, taking you around the fjord and stopping at various islands along the way. You'll have the opportunity to enjoy stunning views, visit charming coastal villages, and learn about the area's history and culture.

Island Hopping: The fjord is dotted with numerous islands, each with its own character and attractions. Some popular islands to explore include Hovedøya, Gressholmen, and Langøyene. These islands offer beautiful beaches, hiking trails, picnic spots, and even camping facilities.

Boating on the oslo fjord

One popular option is kayaking, where guided tours allow you to explore the fjord and Oslo's waterfront while getting a great workout. Companies like Mad Goats Paddling, Oslo By Kayak, Learn2 Kayak, and Oslo Kayak Tours offer kayak tours and courses for various skill levels.

For a Viking experience, you can rent a traditional færing, a Norwegian rowboat, from Åretak near the Opera house. These boats are built using techniques similar to those used for Viking ships. No belief in Norse mythology is required; you just need to know how to swim.

If you prefer a more leisurely experience, you can go on a cruise and relax while exploring the Oslo Fjord. There are options like Trollcruise AS, Brim Explorer, Båtservice Sightseeing, Fjord cruise with Christian Radich, The Fjords, KOK Oslo, RIB Oslo, and Island hopping in the Oslo Fjord. Each offers a unique boating experience, whether it's on a RIB (rigid inflatable boat), electric ferry, old sailing boat, or solar-powered boat.

In addition to boating activities, there are other fjord-related options to explore. Sauna life by the Oslo Fjord is a popular urban sauna culture, and you can also enjoy fjord sightseeing tours and mini cruises. Don't miss out on exploring the beautiful attractions along the Akerselva river or the hidden gems in Oslo's backyards.

Troll Cruise:

Trollcruise specializes in crafting unique boating adventures on the Oslofjord. They curate a variety of events on sailing ships, fjord boats, and eco-friendly yachts (electric boats), complete with professional crews and catering services. These exceptional experiences are open to corporations, individuals, and various groups.

Mad Goats Paddling (new):

Mad Goats Paddling is a kayak tour company located at Nordre gate 2, Oslo, 0551. They provide exciting kayak tours along the Akerselva River and offer courses on the Oslo Fjord. These tours cater to both beginners and experienced paddlers. Additionally, they offer kayaking license courses (våttkort introkurs) that are mandatory for those wanting to paddle on the Oslo Fjord.

Other tips include:

1. Viking Biking & Hiking offers guided tours by bike and on foot.
2. Norway Yacht Charter provides chartered boat trips on the Oslo Fjord, accommodating up to 500 passengers on elegant sailing boats and yachts.
3. Oslo Fjord Sauna offers sauna rafts at Sørenga wharf.
4. Brim Explorer provides eco-friendly boat cruises and tours in the Oslo Fjord.
5. Båtservice Sightseeing offers guided boat tours in Oslo throughout the year, departing from City Hall Pier 3. They have a 2-hour Fjord Sightseeing tour available.
6. Mad Goats Kayak and SUP rental offers kayak and stand-up paddle board rentals.
7. KOK Oslo offers floating saunas in the Oslo Fjord and tours with solar-powered boats.
8. RIB Oslo, located in Tjuvholmen, offers thrilling RIB (rigid inflatable boat) experiences on the fjord all year round.

9. "The part-time monk" provides guided tours of the monastery ruins on the island of Hovedøya.

10. Oslo Fjord Boat Fishing offers guided fishing tours in the northern part of the Oslo Fjord on their Quicksilver boats.

11. Island hopping in the Oslo Fjord is possible by taking a ferry and exploring the inner islands.

12. Fishing in the Oslo Fjord is permitted without a license in the inner part of the fjord, which has many good fishing spots.

13. There is a bicycle route from the city center to Nordstrand Bad, a bathing spot where you can enjoy a swim.

14. Bærum Maritime Senter offers kayak rentals between March and November, with a wide selection of kayaks available.

15. Friluftshuset is an activity and information center operated by the Oslo chapter of DNT (The Norwegian Trekking Association).

16. Oslo Fjordfiske offers guided fishing trips by boat in the Oslo Fjord.

17. Oslo Kayak Tours offers group kayak tours in the scenic surroundings of the Oslo Fjord, suitable for all skill levels.

18. Langøyene, a small island near the city center, has beach volleyball courts available for public use.

19. Sørenga Seawater Pool is a large seawater fjord pool located in one of Oslo's new neighborhoods.

Islands and attractions

Explore the islands of the Oslo Fjord and discover their various attractions, including beautiful beaches, hiking trails, and cultural sites. One notable attraction is the monastery ruins at Hovedøya, which date back to the Middle Ages and provide an exciting experience for visitors of all ages. *Other islands worth visiting include;*

Steilene: located outside Nesodden, offers beaches, a guest harbor, and a lighthouse. Aker Brygge wharf is a popular area along the inner harbor, known for its restaurants, shopping options, and renovated buildings. Langøyene island is accessible by ferry during the summer and features a large beach, a shop, a nudist beach, and a beach volleyball court.

Bleikøya: A small island with numerous summer cottages and a nature reserve, while Ingierstrand beach, located just outside Oslo on the east side of the fjord, is a family-friendly beach with a stunning diving tower and facilities. Gressholmen, Heggholmen, and Rambergøya are three interconnected islands offering great swimming and sunbathing opportunities.

Hovedøya island: The closest island to the city center and boasts beautiful forests, beaches, and cultural heritage sites. Lindøya island, a 15-20 minute ferry ride from the city, is a picturesque island with around 300 summer cottages in vibrant colors. Nakholmen island is home to nearly 200 private summer cottages accessible by ferry from the city center, and Ormøya and Malmøya islands, located east of the city center, can be reached by bus and feature Solvikbukta, a pleasant sandy beach.

Food and Dining

- Seafood: Norway is renowned for its fresh seafood, and Oslo Fjord offers a fantastic opportunity to indulge in delicious dishes. Look for restaurants and cafes that serve traditional Norwegian seafood, such as salmon, shrimp, and cod.
- Local Cuisine: Explore the local cuisine and try traditional Norwegian dishes like rakfisk (fermented fish), lutefisk (dried fish), or fårikål (mutton stew). You can find these specialties in various restaurants throughout Oslo.

Restaurants located near the Oslo Fjord

1. Ingierstrand Restaurant: This summer restaurant is housed in a historic building renowned for its Norwegian functionalist architecture. It caters to boaters and swimmers, providing delicious meals and a charming ambiance.

2. Klosterkroa café: Situated on Hovedøya Island, a short ferry ride away from Oslo's center, Klosterkroa offers snacks during the summer. It's a perfect spot to relax and enjoy the surroundings.

3. Anne på landet – Hvervenbukta: Located next to the beach at Hvervenbukta, this cozy café serves refreshing beverages during the summer and serves hot food and drinks in the winter. It's a great place to unwind.

4. Sjøflyhavna Kro: Situated on the water's edge at Fornebu, Sjøflyhavna Kro is an informal diner housed in a restored historic building. Its maritime atmosphere and retrospective environment make it a unique dining experience.

5. Lille Herbern: Dating back to 1929, Lille Herbern is a restaurant situated on a picturesque island near Bygdøy. It's only open during the summer and offers a charming dining experience.

6. Gressholmen Kro: Located on the island of Gressholmen, this summer café and restaurant has a rich history dating back to 1930. It offers a tranquil setting and is perfect for a peaceful meal.

7. Revierhavnen Kro: Situated on Hovedøya Island in the Oslo Fjord, Revierhavnen Kro is an à la carte restaurant open from Easter to October. Its menu changes with the seasons, ensuring fresh and diverse dining options.

Accommodations in oslo fjord

- Kjeholmen - A self-service cabin on Kjeholmen island with beds for 10 people and additional space.

- Butikken, Nordre Langåra - A newly restored self-service cabin on an island, providing accommodation for up to 20 people.

- Vestli - A self-service cabin on the western side of Nesoddlandet, offering one bedroom with beds for four people.

- Ommen - Two self-service cabins on the Nesodden peninsula, adjacent to the Oslo Fjord, with the main house having five bedrooms.

- Rødstua - A self-service cabin situated in a large recreational area at Nesoddtangen Farm, featuring one bedroom.

- Ytre Vassholmen - A self-service summer house located on Ytre Vassholmen island in the Oslo Fjord.

Nearby Attractions

Oslo City Center: Don't miss the chance to explore the vibrant city of Oslo itself. Visit the Royal Palace, stroll through Vigeland Park, explore the charming streets of the Grünerløkka district, and take in the modern architecture at the Oslo Opera House.

Holmenkollen: Head to the Holmenkollen neighborhood, located just outside Oslo, to visit the famous Holmenkollen Ski Jump

CHAPTER 6:

Oslo city center

Karl Johans Gate

Karl Johans Gate, located in Oslo, Norway, is a vibrant and iconic street that holds great historical, cultural, and architectural significance. Spanning approximately 1.3 kilometers, With its rich history, stunning architecture, and diverse offerings, Karl Johans Gate is a must-visit destination that encapsulates the essence of Oslo.

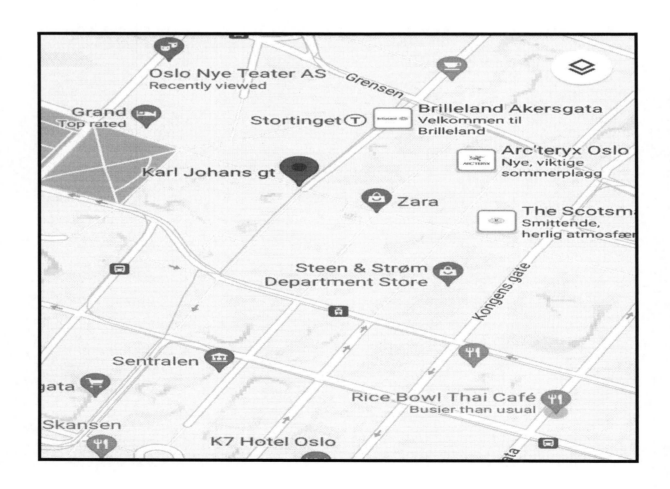

The street was named after King Charles III John, who ruled Norway and Sweden in the early 19th century. It was originally constructed in 1904-1907. Over the years, Karl Johans Gate has witnessed significant transformations, reflecting the changing face of Oslo. Despite these changes, it has managed to retain its charm and character.

One of the prominent landmarks along Karl Johans Gate is the Oslo Central Station, a grand neoclassical building that serves as a major transportation hub. Its architecture blends elements of Gothic Revival and Renaissance Revival styles, making it an architectural marvel. From the station, visitors can enter Karl Johans Gate and embark on a captivating journey.

As you walk along the street, you will be greeted by an eclectic mix of shops, restaurants, cafes, and cultural institutions. High-end boutiques, fashion chains, and local shops line the avenue, offering a wide range of products and experiences. From traditional Norwegian crafts and clothing to international brands, Karl Johans Gate caters to every taste and budget. For art enthusiasts, the street boasts of several notable attractions. The National Theatre, situated halfway along Karl Johans Gate, is a cultural landmark known for its theatrical performances, including those by Henrik Ibsen, Norway's famous playwright. Additionally, the National Gallery is home to an impressive collection of Norwegian and international artworks, including Edvard Munch's iconic painting "The Scream."

Further up the street, you will find the Stortinget, the Norwegian Parliament building. With its neoclassical facade and majestic presence, it symbolizes the nation's democratic values. Visitors can explore the building through guided tours and learn about Norway's political system.

Continuing along Karl Johans Gate, you'll reach the Royal Palace at the end of the street. The palace, built in the 19th century, is the official residence of the Norwegian monarch. While the interior is not open to the public, the surrounding park, known as Slottsparken, offers a serene and picturesque setting for leisurely walks or picnics. From the palace grounds, visitors can also enjoy panoramic views of Oslo's skyline.

Throughout the year, Karl Johans Gate hosts numerous events and celebrations. In May, the street comes alive during the National Day celebrations, when Norwegians commemorate their independence. The vibrant parade, filled with flag-waving locals, passes through the avenue, creating a festive atmosphere. During the winter season, Karl Johans Gate transforms into a magical wonderland adorned with festive decorations and twinkling lights, attracting visitors to explore its holiday markets and ice-skating rinks.

Nasjonal jazzscene - Victoria

Nasjonal jazzscene - Victoria is a well-known national jazz stage located on Karl Johans gate in Oslo. It occupies a former movie theater and presents a diverse and contemporary concert program, showcasing some of the finest jazz talents from Norway and around the world. The concerts are scheduled from Wednesday to Saturday.

The seating arrangement at Victoria is thoughtfully designed to offer an excellent viewing experience from all vantage points. Guests can find café tables near the stage, a four-level sofa amphitheater at the rear, and galleries on both sides. While they offer a good selection of wines, beers, and non-alcoholic beverages at the bar, they do not serve food.

The venue is fully accessible for people with disabilities, featuring appropriately designed toilets and a flexible furniture plan to accommodate wheelchairs. As part of the Norwegian accompanying scheme, Victoria ensures that attendees who require assistance can reach out to them during ticket purchase.

Karl Johans Gate is much more than just a street. It encapsulates the history, culture, and spirit of Oslo. With its architectural splendor, diverse offerings, and proximity to significant landmarks.

Oslo Royal Palace

Address:

The Royal Palace, Slottsplassen 1, 0010 Oslo,Norway.

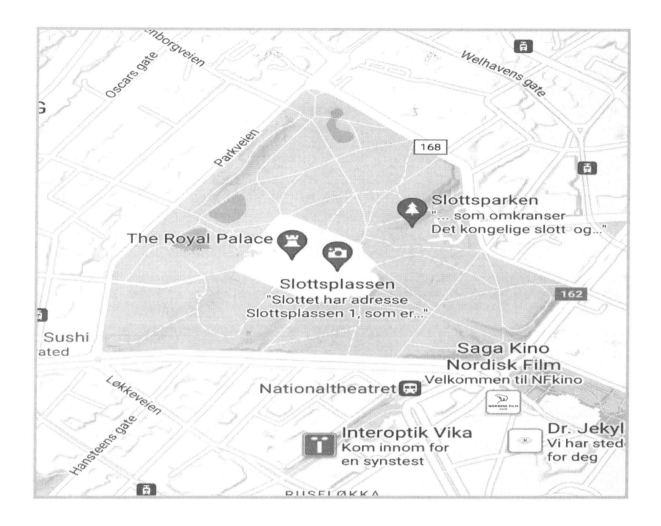

The Royal Palace, located in the heart of Oslo, is used for state visits, official functions, and as the workplace for the King and Queen. The Royal palace also serves as the venue for various royal events and official functions.

The Royal Palace was built in the first half of the 19th century and completed in 1849. It was initially designed by the Norwegian architect Hans Linstow in a neoclassical architectural style, with some inspiration from French and Italian Renaissance palaces. The palace has undergone several renovations and additions over the years, including a major reconstruction after a fire in 1859.

The Royal Palace is an impressive building with a grand facade adorned with columns and statues. It features a large central block with two wings extending on either side. The palace is surrounded by a beautiful park called Palace Park, which is open to the public and a popular spot for leisurely walks.

While the Royal Palace is the official residence of the Norwegian monarch, King Harald V, and Queen Sonja, they actually reside at the nearby Skaugum Estate in Asker, outside of Oslo.

Opening Hours and Access:

The Oslo Royal Palace is open for public tours during the summer season. Usually 9am to 4pm, daily. However, exact dates and timings may vary, so it's recommended to check the official website or contact the Palace in advance.

Access to the interior of the Palace is only possible through guided tours, including the Bird Room, the Great Hall, and the Council Chamber. The palace also houses an art collection, showcasing works by renowned Norwegian artists. Book your tickets in advance to secure a spot.

Touring the Interior:

- The guided tours typically last for about one hour and cover several rooms and halls within the Palace.
- You'll have the opportunity to explore the staterooms, where official receptions and ceremonies take place. Admire the exquisite decor, intricate details, and artwork on display.

- The tour may also include visits to the Banqueting Hall, Council Chamber, and other significant spaces within the Palace.
- During the tour, knowledgeable guides will provide interesting insights into the history, architecture, and royal traditions associated with the Palace.

Changing of the Guard:

- One of the highlights of visiting the Royal Palace is witnessing the Changing of the Guard ceremony.
- The ceremony takes place daily at 11:30 am and lasts for about 40 minutes. Arriving a bit earlier will allow you to secure a good viewing spot.
- The event features a marching band, guards on horseback, and a meticulously choreographed routine that adds pomp and grandeur to the experience.

Exploring the Grounds:

- The Palace is surrounded by beautiful gardens and green spaces that are open to the public.
- Take a stroll through the Palace Park, enjoy the serene atmosphere, and appreciate the well-maintained landscapes.
- Keep an eye out for the Palace Guards stationed around the grounds, and you might even catch a glimpse of the royal family if they are in residence.

Oslo City Hall

Location:

Oslo City Hall, or Oslo Rådhus in Norwegian, is located in the city center of Oslo, Norway. It sits on the waterfront of the Oslo Fjord, near the Aker Brygge district. The address is Rådhusplassen 1, 0037 Oslo, Norway.

Overview:

Oslo City Hall is an iconic building that serves as the seat of the Oslo City Council and the mayor's office. It was completed in 1950 and is known for its distinctive architecture, featuring a blend of art deco and functionalist styles. The building's interior showcases impressive murals, sculptures, and decorations by various Norwegian artists.

Things to Do and See:

1. City Hall Tours: Guided tours are available to explore the interior of Oslo City Hall. The tours provide insight into the building's history, architecture, and significant artworks. They are usually offered in Norwegian and English.

2. Main Hall: The Main Hall (Festsalen) is the largest room in Oslo City Hall. It is used for official ceremonies, including the Nobel Peace Prize award ceremony held annually on December 10th. The hall is adorned with beautiful murals depicting scenes from Norwegian history.

3. Oslo City Hall Gallery: The Gallery (Galleriet) is located on the second floor and showcases a rotating exhibition of contemporary art by Norwegian artists. It's a great place to discover the works of local talents.

4. The Great Hall: The Great Hall (Store Sal) is another impressive space within the City Hall, known for its grandeur and exquisite artwork. It houses a giant mural named "The Life of the People" by renowned Norwegian artist Henrik Sørensen.

5. City Hall Square: Outside the building, you can explore the City Hall Square (Rådhusplassen). It offers a panoramic view of the Oslo Fjord and is a popular spot for events, festivals, and public gatherings.

Tips for Visiting:

Opening Hours: Oslo City Hall is generally open to the public from 9:00 AM to 16:00 PM, daily. However, opening hours may vary due to official functions or events.

Guided Tours:

If you want to take a guided tour, it's advisable to book in advance, especially during peak tourist seasons. Information about tours and booking can be found on the official Oslo City Hall website.

Accessibility:

The City Hall is wheelchair accessible, with ramps and elevators available for easy movement within the building. If you have any specific accessibility needs, it's recommended to contact them beforehand to ensure a smooth visit.

Photography:

The use of flash photography is now allowed in most areas of the City Hall, except in the Main Hall. However, the use of flash and tripods may be restricted.

Aker Brygge

Aker Brygge, one of Oslo's most popular waterfront areas! Aker Brygge is a vibrant district located on the western side of the city center, known for its stunning harbor views, trendy shops, restaurants, and cultural attractions.

Location and Getting There:

The exact address of Aker Brygge is Stranden 1, 0250 Oslo, Norway. It is easily accessible by public transportation, including buses, trams, and ferries. The closest metro station is the National Theatre, which is within walking distance.

Exploring the Area:

- Start by taking a leisurely stroll along the waterfront promenade. Enjoy the scenic views of the harbor and watch boats sailing by.

- Explore the Tjuvholmen Park, a beautiful park adjacent to Aker Brygge that offers stunning views of the Oslo Fjord.

- Visit the Astrup Fearnley Museum, which relocated to Tjuvholmen in 2012 and houses contemporary art exhibitions.

- Visit the Tjuvholmen Skulpturpark, an outdoor sculpture park with intriguing sculptures.

- Embark on a boat tour of the Oslo Fjord to experience the city from a different perspective and enjoy the picturesque surroundings.

Shopping:

- Aker Brygge is home to several upscale shops and boutiques. You'll find international brands, high-end fashion, and local Norwegian designers.
- Explore the Aker Brygge Shopping Mall, which offers a range of stores catering to different tastes and interests.
- For unique Norwegian souvenirs and handicrafts, visit the local shops and market stalls scattered throughout the area.

Dining and Nightlife:

- Aker Brygge boasts numerous restaurants, cafes, and bars that offer diverse cuisines and atmospheres. From seafood to international dishes, you'll find something to suit your taste.
- Enjoy a meal with a view by choosing a restaurant with outdoor seating overlooking the harbor.
- The area also comes alive at night with lively bars and clubs.

Activities and Entertainment:

Explore the Promenade: Start your visit by taking a stroll along the promenade that stretches along the waterfront. Enjoy the fresh sea breeze, admire the boats and yachts, and take in the picturesque views of the fjord.

- Take a boat tour or hop on a ferry from Aker Brygge to explore the Oslo Fjord and its islands. It's a great way to enjoy the stunning scenery and learn about the city's maritime history.
- During the summer months, you can find pop-up street performances and festivals along the waterfront, adding to the lively atmosphere.

Nearby Attractions:

- Visit the Nobel Peace Center, located just a short walk from Aker Brygge. It provides an in-depth exploration of the Nobel Peace Prize and its laureates.
- Take a leisurely walk to the Akershus Fortress, a medieval castle, and fortress that offers panoramic views of Oslo and the fjord.
- Explore the vibrant neighborhood of Tjuvholmen, which is adjacent to Aker Brygge. It features more art galleries, trendy cafes, and the famous Thief Spa.

Akershus Fortress

Akershus Fortress, also known as Akershus Castle, is a historic fortress located in Oslo, Norway. It has a rich history dating back to the 13th century and is a popular tourist attraction.

Location and Opening Hours:

Akershus Fortress is situated in the heart of Oslo, overlooking the Oslo Fjord. The exact address is Akershus Festning, 0150 Oslo, Norway. The fortress is open to the public throughout the year.

Getting There:

Akershus Fortress is easily accessible from various parts of Oslo. You can reach it by public transportation, such as buses, trams, or ferries.

The nearest tram stop is Aker, and several buses also stop nearby. If you prefer walking, it's a pleasant stroll from the city center, taking approximately 10-15 minutes.

Guided Tours:

To gain deeper insights into the fortress's history and significance, consider joining a guided tour. The fortress offers guided tours in multiple languages, providing fascinating details about its architecture, medieval roots, and the role it played in Norwegian history. Check the official website for the tour schedule and booking information.

Exploring the Fortress:

Akershus Fortress offers a variety of attractions to explore:

Castle Grounds:

Take a leisurely walk through the fortress's extensive grounds. Enjoy the beautiful views of the Oslo Fjord, wander along the fortress walls, and relax in the serene surroundings.

Akershus Castle:

Visit the historic castle, which now serves as a museum. Explore the various rooms and exhibitions that showcase the castle's history, including medieval artifacts, weaponry, and artwork. Don't miss the stunning Great Hall, the Royal Mausoleum, or the dungeons.

Norwegian Resistance and Freedom Museum: The Norwegian Resistance Museum is also located inside Akershus Fortress. It focuses on Norway's resistance movement during World War II and provides a comprehensive overview of the country's occupation history.

Events and Festivities:

Akershus Fortress is a vibrant location for various cultural events and festivals throughout the year. Keep an eye on the local event calendar to see if any festivals, concerts, or historical reenactments coincide with your visit.

Nearby Attractions:

When you visit Akershus Fortress, you'll find several other attractions within walking distance. Consider exploring Oslo City Hall, Aker Brygge, the Royal Palace, or taking a stroll along Karl Johans Gate, Oslo's main street.

Remember to dress comfortably and wear appropriate footwear, as there might be some walking involved during your visit to the fortress. Also, check the weather forecast beforehand and bring necessary items like an umbrella or sunscreen, depending on the season.

Oslo opera house

The Oslo Opera House is one of the most iconic landmarks in Oslo, known for its stunning architecture and world-class performances.

Location and Opening Hours:

The Oslo Opera House is located in the Bjørvika neighborhood, at Kirsten Flagstads Plass 1, 0150 Oslo, Norway. It is situated right by the waterfront, offering beautiful views of the Oslo Fjord. The opening hours vary depending on performances, so it's best to check the official website for the current schedule.

Architecture and Design:

The Opera House is renowned for its modern and distinctive design. It resembles an iceberg floating on the water, with its sloping roof that allows visitors to walk on top. The marble-clad exterior and large glass windows create a visually striking building. The interior is equally impressive, featuring grand auditoriums and elegant spaces.

Guided Tours:

To explore the Opera House more thoroughly, consider joining a guided tour. These tours provide behind-the-scenes insights into the building, including the backstage areas, rehearsal rooms, and costume workshops.

Performances:

Attending a performance at the Opera House is a must-do experience. The venue hosts a wide range of operas, ballets, concerts, and other cultural events throughout the year. The program includes both Norwegian and international productions, featuring talented artists and musicians. Be sure to check the schedule in advance and book tickets accordingly.

Ticket Booking:

Tickets for performances can be purchased online through the Opera House's official website or at the box office. Popular shows tend to sell out quickly, so it's advisable to book in advance. The website provides detailed information about each performance, including seat maps, ticket prices, and availability.

Dress Code:

There is no strict dress code at the Opera House, but many visitors prefer to dress smartly for evening performances. It's common to see people wearing elegant attire, such as dresses, suits, or business casual outfits. However, for daytime tours or casual events, comfortable clothing is perfectly acceptable.

Nearby Attractions:

While visiting the Opera House, take the opportunity to explore other nearby attractions. The Astrup Fearnley Museum of Modern Art and the Munch Museum are within walking distance. You can also enjoy a stroll along the Oslo waterfront promenade or visit the historical Oslo Fortress, Akershus Castle.

Photography:

Photography is generally allowed in the public areas of the Opera House. However, during performances, photography and recording devices are not permitted.

Foyer and Restaurants:

The Opera House's foyer is an expansive space where visitors can relax, enjoy refreshments, and soak in the vibrant atmosphere The Opera House has a restaurant and bar on the ground floor, offering a variety of dining options. You can indulge in Norwegian cuisine while enjoying the elegant surroundings. Additionally, there are several cafes and restaurants in the nearby Aker Brygge area, where you can savor a range of international and local culinary delights.

Accessibility:

The Opera House is designed to be accessible to all visitors. It has ramps and elevators for easy access, and wheelchair seating is available in the auditoriums. If you have specific accessibility requirements, it's recommended to contact the Opera House in advance to ensure a smooth and comfortable visit.

Oslo Opera House Roof Walk:

Walk on the Opera House's roof. It's free and open to the public, providing a unique perspective of the city. You can ascend the sloping marble surfaces and enjoy breathtaking views of Oslo and the fjord.

Deichman Bjørvika library

The library is located in the Bjørvika district of Oslo, next to the Opera House. The library building was designed by Norwegian architectural firms Lundhagem Arkitekter and Atelier Oslo and opened in June 2020. It has six floors and is home to a collection of more than one million books, newspapers, magazines, and other materials. The library also offers a variety of programs and services, including:

- Reading and study areas
- Computer stations
- Meeting rooms
- Children's areas
- Cafés
- Events and workshops
- The Future Library, an art project that collects one manuscript a year from 100 authors over a period of 100 years. The manuscripts are stored in the library and will not be published until 2114.

Tips for visiting the Deichman Bjørvika library:

- Book your tickets in advance, especially if you are visiting during peak season.
- Allow plenty of time to explore the library, as there is a lot to see.
- Wear comfortable shoes, as you will be doing a lot of walking.
- Take advantage of the library's many educational resources, such as the audio guide and the children's activities.
- Be sure to visit the Future Library to see the manuscripts from the 100 authors.

Rose Castle art installation

The Rose Castle is a large-scale art installation on Holmenkollen near Frognerseteren that commemorates 80 years since the attack on Norway in 1940 and the 75th anniversary of Norway's liberation in 1945. The installation was created by the Norwegian artists Vebjørn Sand and Eimund Sand and was opened in 2020.

The Rose Castle is made up of a series of sculptures, paintings, and sound and light installations that tell the story of the occupation of Norway during World War II. The installation is designed to be a place of reflection and remembrance, and it is a powerful reminder of the importance of freedom and democracy.

The Rose Castle is open to the public from June to September. Tickets can be purchased online or at the ticket office on site. The installation is located at Frognerseteren, 0791 Oslo.

Here are some tips for visiting the Rose Castle:

- Book your tickets in advance, especially if you are visiting during peak season.
- Allow plenty of time to explore the installation, as there is a lot to see.
- Wear comfortable shoes, as you will be doing a lot of walking.
- Take advantage of the audio guide to learn more about the installation.
- Be sure to visit the Rose Gate, which is the entrance to the installation. The gate is made up of five meters of roses, which represent the five years of the occupation.

- Visit the Rose Tower, which offers panoramic views of Oslo and the surrounding area.
- Visit the Rose Hall, which is a space for reflection and remembrance. The hall is filled with sculptures and paintings that depict the horrors of war.

Oslo National Theatre

Oslo National Theatre, also known as Det Norske Teatret, is a prominent cultural institution in Norway. As one of the country's premier theaters, it showcases a wide range of performances, including plays, musicals, ballets, and operas.

Location:

Address: Johanne Dybwads 1, 0161 Oslo

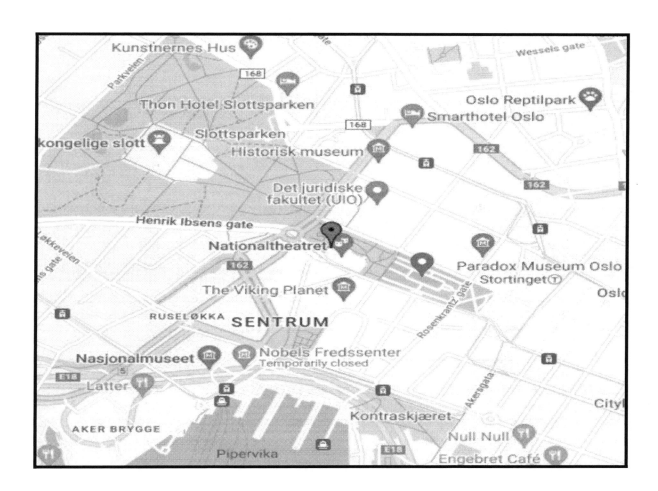

Performance Schedule:

The theater offers performances in Norwegian, so be sure to check if there are any English-language productions or performances with subtitles if you don't understand Norwegian.

Tickets:

Purchase your tickets in advance, especially for popular shows, as they can sell out quickly. You can buy tickets online through the theater's website or visit the box office in person.

Dress Code:

There is no strict dress code at Oslo National Theatre. People generally dress smart-casual or according to the occasion. However, it's always a good idea to dress a bit more formally for evening performances.

Pre-show Dining:

The theater is located in an area with numerous dining options. If you're looking for a pre-show meal, you can find a variety of restaurants and cafes in the vicinity. Consider arriving early to enjoy a leisurely dinner before the performance.

The theater comprises four stages, namely the Main Stage (Hovedscenen), the Amphitheater (Amfiscenen), the Painting Gallery (Malerasalen), and the Torshov Theatre (Torshovteatret).

Within the theater, you will find several ensembles, such as the Nationaltheatret Ensemble, the Ung Scene Ensemble, and the Torshovteatret Ensemble.

Additionally, the theater provides an array of educational opportunities, including workshops, lectures, and guided tours as part of their educational programs.

Guided Tours:

Oslo National Theatre offers guided tours that provide insight into the history, architecture, and behind-the-scenes aspects of the theater. If you're interested in learning more about the institution, consider joining one of these tours.

Accessibility:

The theater is equipped with facilities for individuals with disabilities, including accessible entrances, wheelchair seating, and accessible restrooms. Contact the theater in advance if you require any specific accommodations.

Souvenirs:

The theater usually has a small shop where you can purchase theater-related souvenirs, such as books, posters, and other memorabilia.

Oslo Cathedral,

Also known as Oslo Domkirke or the Cathedral of St. Hallvard.

Location and Opening Hours:

Oslo Cathedral is situated in the city center at Karl Johans gate 11, 0154 Oslo, Norway.

The opening hours vary depending on the time of year and services, so it's recommended to check the official website or contact the cathedral for the most up-to-date information.

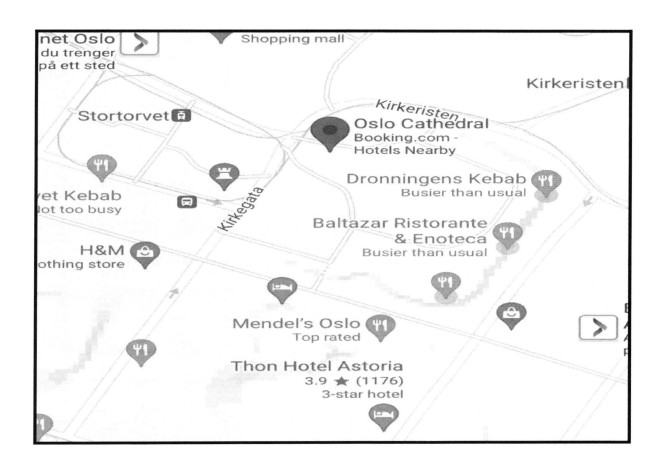

History and Significance:

Oslo Cathedral dates back to the 11th century when it was originally constructed as a small wooden church. Over the years, the cathedral has undergone several renovations and expansions, resulting in its present-day neo-Gothic architectural style. The cathedral plays a central role in religious ceremonies, including royal weddings, funerals, and national events.

Architecture and Interior:

Oslo Cathedral showcases impressive neo-Gothic architecture with intricate detailing, pointed arches, and stunning stained glass windows.
The interior features a serene and elegant atmosphere, with beautiful decorations, religious art, and ornate altars.

Guided Tours:

Oslo Cathedral offers guided tours that provide deeper insights into its history, art, and significance. These tours are usually available in Norwegian and English and are led by knowledgeable guides who can provide interesting anecdotes and answer any questions you may have. Check the cathedral's official website for tour schedules and availability.

Services and Events:

The cathedral is an active place of worship and holds regular church services. Additionally, Oslo Cathedral hosts various cultural events, including concerts and organ recitals. Keep an eye out for any special events happening during your stay.

Practical Information:

- Admission: Entry to the Oslo Cathedral is generally free, although donations are welcome to support its upkeep.
- Opening Hours: The cathedral is typically open to the public from morning until evening. Note that during services and events, access may be restricted.
- Photography: Photography is generally allowed inside the cathedral, but be respectful of any restrictions during religious services or events.
- Dress Code: As a place of worship, it is advisable to dress modestly when visiting the cathedral.

Vigeland Sculpture Park

Vigeland Sculpture Park, also known as Frogner Park, is one of the most popular attractions in Oslo, Norway. It is located in the Frogner neighborhood, just a short distance northwest of the city center. The park covers an area of 80 acres and is home to over 200 sculptures created by the renowned Norwegian artist Gustav Vigeland.

Location:

Frogner Park is situated at Kirkeveien 0268, Oslo, Norway. It's easily accessible by public transportation, including buses, trams, and the metro. The nearest metro station is Majorstuen.

Opening Hours:

The park is open 24 hours a day, all year round, and admission is free. However, the Vigeland Museum located within the park has specific opening hours.

Highlights:

The main highlight of Vigeland Sculpture Park is the impressive display of Gustav Vigeland's sculptures. The most iconic sculpture is the Monolith, a towering 46-feet high granite column carved with intertwined human figures. Other notable sculptures include the Angry Boy, the Wheel of Life, and the Fountain.

Vigeland Museum:

Inside the park, you'll find the Vigeland Museum, which showcases the life and works of Gustav Vigeland. The museum provides deeper insights into the artist's creative process and features a collection of his sketches, models, and sculptures.

Exploring the Park:

Take your time to wander through the park's beautifully landscaped grounds. The sculptures are spread throughout the park, and there are several pathways that lead you through different sections. Enjoy the serene atmosphere and the artistry of Vigeland's sculptures as you stroll along.

Activities:

Vigeland Sculpture Park is a popular spot for picnicking, jogging, and relaxing. Many locals and visitors come here to enjoy the expansive lawns, gardens, and tranquil settings. You'll often find people engaging in various recreational activities, especially during the summer months.

Facilities:

The park offers facilities such as public restrooms, benches, and a café where you can grab a snack or a cup of coffee. The Vigeland Museum also has its own café and a gift shop.

Nearby Attractions:

If you have time, you can explore other attractions in the vicinity of Frogner Park. These include the Royal Palace, Aker Brygge waterfront area, and the Museum of Cultural History.

The park can be quite busy during weekends and holidays, so visiting during weekdays or early morning hours can provide a more peaceful experience.

Skimore Oslo

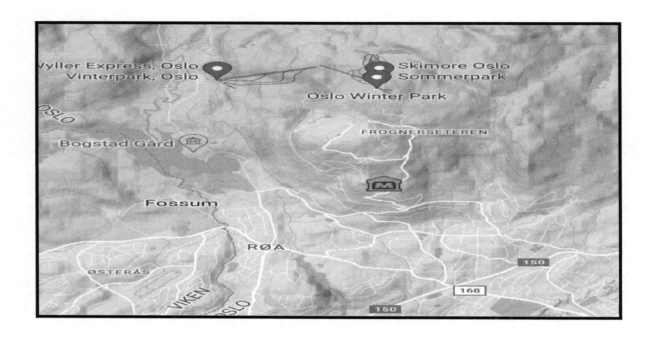

Skimore Oslo Summer Park is one of the largest climbing parks in Scandinavia, conveniently located just half an hour away from Oslo's city center. The park offers a thrilling experience with its 12 trails of varying difficulty levels, featuring over 200 elements such as zip lines, bridges, and tunnels. Safety is a top priority, and all visitors receive necessary equipment and training to enjoy a safe day high up in the treetops.

Location and Opening hours:

Address: Skigardsveien 50 1405 Langhus, Oslo.

The park operates with different opening hours depending on the month:

- In July and August, it's open from Monday to Saturday, 8:30 am to 6 pm, and on Sundays from 9 am to 5 pm.
- During June and September, it opens on Saturdays and Sundays from 10 am to 5 pm, and on Tuesdays from 12 pm to 8 pm.

As for the pricing, the park offers various options:

- Adults (16+ years) can purchase a pass for NOK 320.
- Children (ages 4-15) have a reduced price of NOK 220.
- Families consisting of two adults and two children can opt for a family ticket at NOK 840.

There are also some discounts available:

- Oslo Pass holders receive a 15% discount on drop-in climbing passes on weekdays.
- Children under 4 years old can enter the park for free.

With all the exciting activities and options available, Skimore Oslo – Summer Park provides an excellent destination for a fun-filled and adventurous day out in nature.

Sentralen

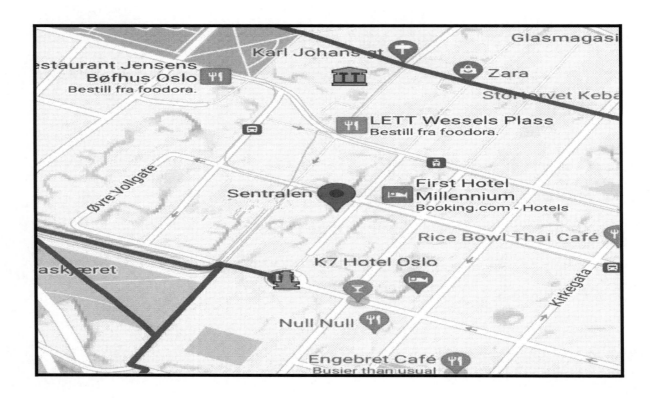

Location:

Sentralen is located in the Kvadraturen section of downtown Oslo. The exact address is: **Øvre Slottsgate 3, 0157 Oslo, Norway**

The historic building of Norway's oldest savings bank, located in the heart of Oslo's city center, has been transformed into an exceptional cultural hub known as Sentralen. With six stages, it hosts a diverse range of cultural performances and activities. Visitors can also enjoy a restaurant and café with delectable dishes prepared by renowned chefs.

Sentralen not only hosts cultural events but also provides rehearsal and production spaces, as well as attractive meeting and conference facilities available for rental. The building serves as a workplace for over 350 creative individuals working in various cultural fields.

Sparebankstiftelsen DNB fully financed the restoration of this old building, which is now owned by them.

For environmentally conscious visitors, Sentralen is environmentally certified as part of Green Oslo..

The harbor promenade

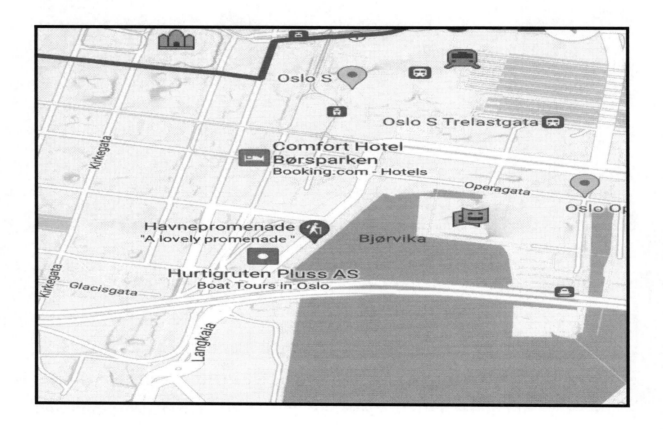

Location

The Oslo Promenade is a waterfront walkway situated in the heart of Oslo, Norway. It extends approximately 1.5 kilometers (0.93 mi) along the Oslofjord, stretching from the Royal Palace to the Opera House.

The precise location of the Oslo Promenade can be found at Rådhusgata 1, 0158 Oslo, Norway, with GPS coordinates 59.914305, 10.738931. To access the promenade, you can utilize various modes of public transportation:

- T-bane: Travel to the National theatret station, which provides convenient access to the promenade.
- Bus: Alight at the Rådhusgata stop, which is in close proximity to the promenade.
- Ferry: Take advantage of the ferry services available, disembarking at the Opera House stop.

Oslo promenade offers a unique urban adventure, combining natural beauty with architecture, art, and delicious food. It was once unimaginable to walk along the fjord from Sørenga to Frognerkilen without interruption, but now the promenade is complete with parks, wharves, and comfortable benches.

The promenade connects the old and new parts of the city, providing a range of experiences for cyclists, tourists, walkers, and those seeking leisurely strolls. It's recommended to wear comfortable shoes for this journey of discovery. To guide your way, 14 large orange lighthouses have been placed along the entire stretch, each adorned with art and informative boards about the surrounding areas.

Start your trip at Sørenga, a new district with stunning views of the Oslo Fjord and the city. Paddlers can enjoy the illuminated paddling tunnel that runs under Oslo S and out into Akerselva.

Cross the footbridge towards the Opera House and witness how the city seamlessly integrates with the fjord. At Sukkerbiten, explore Oslo Fjordhage (known as "The Dome"), floating saunas, and the cozy bar on the converted boat, MS Bjørvika.

Consider making a detour to the brand new MUNCH museum, where you can also explore the charming houses in Bispevika and enjoy the playful water jets. Before continuing, grab some coffee and donuts at Talormade.

Embark on an architecture safari in Bjørvika, where you'll encounter landmarks such as the Opera House, Deichman Bjørvika (the library), and the Barcode high-rises. Stroll over the Opera roof, immerse yourself in books at Deichman, and capture the intriguing details of the Barcode buildings.

Next, continue along Langkaia and discover SALT, comprising wooden structures filled with art, music, food, and sauna experiences. This hidden gem offers various events and installations throughout the year.

If you're feeling hungry, visit Vippa, a food hall located on the fjord's edge. Indulge in diverse cuisine and admire the artistic decorations both inside and outside the building.

As you progress along Akershusstranda, take a detour to Akershus Fortress and Castle, a historical site that has protected the city since the 14th century. Pass by Oslo Town Hall, the Nobel Peace Center, and the new National Museum. Finally, explore the Tjuvholmen neighborhood, known for its architectural diversity, outdoor spaces, and galleries, including the renowned Astrup Fearnley Museum.

At Filipstadkaia, you'll find Skur 13, a large indoor skate hall adorned with art by Pushwagner. Skate enthusiasts can enjoy the same surface as world stars, and outside the hall, there's exercise equipment, benches, and the Oslo Tree—a spectacular 14-meter artificial tree illuminated by LED lamps.

This journey continues to Kongen Marina and Frognerkilen, where the last orange tower awaits. From there, coastal paths offer a scenic conclusion to your exploration of the harbor promenade.

CHAPTER 7

Museums and Galleries

The Viking Ship Museum

The Viking Ship Museum is a popular tourist destination that showcases the history and artifacts of the Vikings, specifically their well-preserved ships.

Location:

The Viking Ship Museum is situated on the Bygdøy peninsula, which is approximately 3 kilometers (1.9 miles) west of central Oslo. The address is Huk Aveny 35, 0287 Oslo, Norway.

Getting there:

- By public transportation: From Oslo city center, you can take bus number 30 or 31 from Jernbanetorget (near Oslo Central Station) to the Bygdøy stop. From there, it's a short walk to the museum.
- By ferry: Another scenic option is to take a ferry from pier 3 behind Oslo City Hall (Rådhusbrygge 3) to Bygdøynes. The ferry ride takes around 10 minutes, and then it's a 15-minute walk to the museum.

Opening hours:

The Viking ships in Oslo are currently unavailable for public viewing. The Viking Ship Museum, where they were housed, is undergoing a much-needed renovation and is closed. However, a remarkable Museum of the Viking Age is set to open in 2026, boasting a threefold increase in size compared to the previous museum. Despite the expansion, the magnificent ships will remain the primary highlight of the new museum.

Highlights and activities:

- Viking ships: The museum houses three well-preserved Viking ships, including the Oseberg, Gokstad, and Tune ships. These impressive vessels provide insights into Viking seafaring and burial customs.
- Exhibitions: Explore the various exhibitions that showcase Viking artifacts, including tools, household items, and other archaeological finds.
- Guided tours: The museum offers guided tours, which can enhance your understanding of Viking history and provide deeper insights into the exhibits. Check the museum's website for the tour schedules.

Nearby attractions:

Since you'll already be in the Bygdøy peninsula, you might want to explore other attractions in the area, including the Norwegian Folk Museum, the Fram Museum (dedicated to polar exploration), and the Kon-Tiki Museum (focused on Thor Heyerdahl's expeditions).

Amenities:

The Viking Ship Museum has facilities such as a museum shop, a café, and restrooms for visitors' convenience.

The Fram Museum

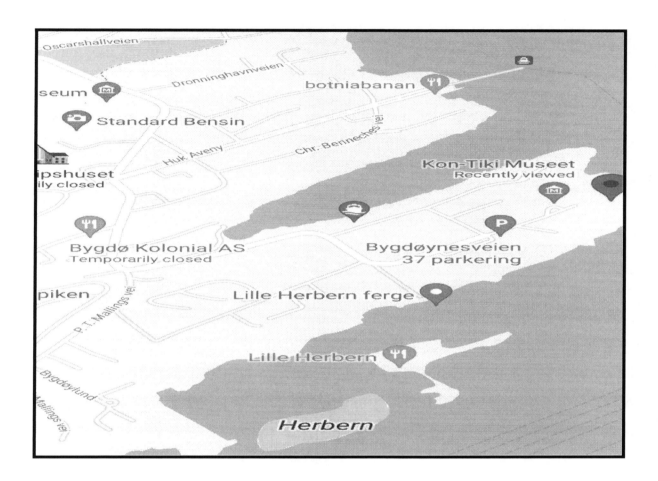

Location:

The Fram Museum is situated on the Bygdøy Peninsula, which is about 10 kilometers from the city center of Oslo. You can reach the museum by public transportation, such as bus or ferry, or by car.

History of the Museum:

The museum was opened in 1936 and is named after the famous Norwegian polar exploration ship, Fram. The Fram was used by several renowned explorers, including Fridtjof Nansen and Roald Amundsen, to navigate the Arctic and Antarctic regions.

Exhibits and Highlights: The museum offers a range of fascinating exhibits that showcase the history of polar exploration. Here are some highlights:

- The Fram: The centerpiece of the museum is the actual polar exploration ship, Fram, which is displayed in its entirety. You can explore the decks, cabins, and cargo holds to get a sense of what life was like for the explorers.

- Exploration History: The museum provides an in-depth look at the history of polar exploration, featuring artifacts, photographs, and interactive displays. Learn about the challenges faced by early explorers and their remarkable achievements.

- Roald Amundsen: Discover the story of Roald Amundsen, the first person to reach the South Pole. Explore his life, expeditions, and the equipment used during his polar adventures.

- Arctic and Antarctic Wildlife: Learn about the unique ecosystems of the Arctic and Antarctic regions, including the diverse wildlife that inhabits these areas. The museum showcases various specimens and provides educational information about the polar environment.

Interactive Experiences:

The Fram Museum offers interactive experiences that allow visitors to engage with the exhibits. You can try your hand at tying knots used by the explorers, experience the freezing temperatures of the polar regions, and even navigate a virtual ship through icy waters.

Guided Tours and Activities:

The museum provides guided tours led by knowledgeable staff who share stories and insights about polar exploration. Additionally, there are often special activities and events for both children and adults, such as lectures, workshops, and film screenings.

Facilities:

The museum has a café where you can enjoy a meal or grab a snack, as well as a gift shop where you can purchase polar exploration-related souvenirs and books.

Nearby Attractions:

While visiting the Fram Museum, you can also explore other attractions on the Bygdøy Peninsula, such as the Kon-Tiki Museum, the Norwegian Maritime Museum, and the Viking Ship Museum.

The Kon-Tiki

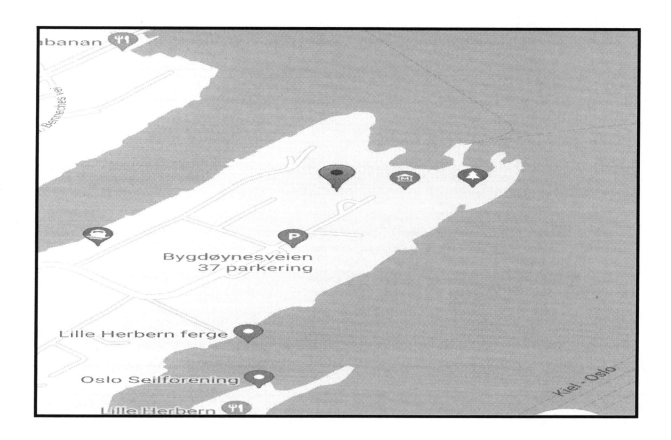

Location and Facilities:

The Kon–Tiki Museum is situated on the Bygdøy Peninsula, which is also home to several other popular museums in Oslo. Specifically at Bygdøynesveien 36, 0286 Oslo, Norway. Once you arrive in the vicinity, you can easily spot the museum, as it is a well-known attraction in Oslo, known for its concentration of cultural and historical attractions. It is easily accessible by public transportation or by ferry from the city center.

Opening hours

Monday to Sunday

November–Apri - 10:00–17:00

May - 10:00–18:00

June–August - 09:30–18:00

September–October - 10:00–17:00

Thor Heyerdahl:

The museum is primarily dedicated to the life and expeditions of Thor Heyerdahl (1914-2002), a Norwegian adventurer, ethnographer, and archaeologist. Heyerdahl gained international fame for his daring expeditions and his theories about ancient seafaring civilizations.

The Kon-Tiki Expedition:

The museum's main attraction is the Kon-Tiki raft, which Heyerdahl and his crew used to sail across the Pacific Ocean from Peru to Polynesia in 1947. The journey aimed to prove Heyerdahl's hypothesis that Polynesia could have been populated by ancient South American cultures. The Kon-Tiki raft itself is on display, allowing visitors to see the vessel up close and appreciate the remarkable feat of the expedition.

Kon-Tiki raft

Exhibits and Artifacts:

Apart from the Kon-Tiki raft, the museum features a wide range of exhibits and artifacts related to Heyerdahl's various expeditions. These include the papyrus boat Ra II, which Heyerdahl used to sail across the Atlantic Ocean from Morocco to Barbados, and the reed boat Tigris, which he sailed from Iraq to Bahrain to highlight ancient trade routes. The museum also houses displays on Easter Island culture, with artifacts and information about Heyerdahl's research there.

Heyerdahl's Legacy:

The museum aims to preserve and promote Thor Heyerdahl's legacy by showcasing his expeditions, theories, and contributions to our understanding of ancient civilizations. Visitors can learn about his passion for exploration, his interdisciplinary approach, and his dedication to challenging established academic views.

Multimedia Presentations:

The Kon-Tiki Museum offers multimedia presentations that enhance the visitor experience. Through films, documentaries, and interactive displays, visitors can delve deeper into the details of Heyerdahl's expeditions, the challenges faced by the crews, and the scientific insights gained from their journeys.

Along with the Kon-Tiki Museum, visitors can explore attractions like the Viking Ship Museum, the Norwegian Folk Museum, and the Fram Museum, which houses the famous polar exploration vessel Fram. The area offers beautiful coastal scenery and walking trails, making it a pleasant destination for a day of cultural and outdoor exploration.

The Nobel Peace Center

The Nobel Peace Center is a prominent museum located in Oslo. It showcases the Nobel Peace Prize laureates and their contributions to promoting peace and resolving conflicts worldwide.

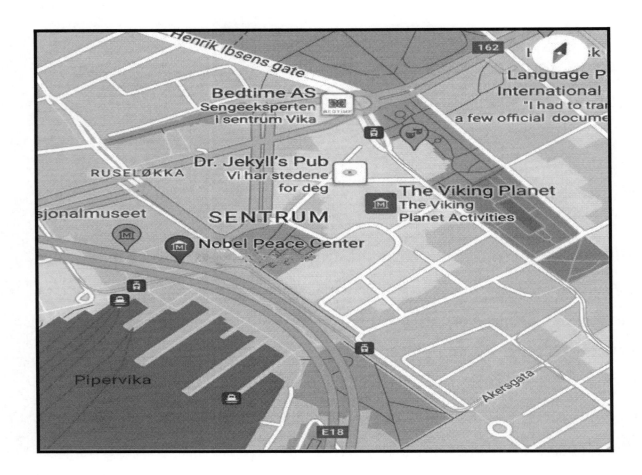

Location:

 The Nobel Peace Center is situated in the heart of Oslo, at Brynjulf Bulls 1, just a short walk from the City Hall and the Aker Brygge waterfront,

Brynjulf Bulls plass 1, 0250 Oslo.

Opening Hours:

The museum is typically open from 10:00 AM to 6:00 PM on weekdays, and 11:00 AM to 6:00 PM on weekends. However, it's always a good idea to check their official website before setting out, or contact them directly for the most up-to-date information on opening hours.

Exhibitions:

The Nobel Peace Center offers engaging and interactive exhibitions that focus on the Nobel Peace Prize laureates, their work, and the impact they have made in various fields. The exhibitions often cover topics such as human rights, conflict resolution, environmental issues, and disarmament.

Guided Tours:

The museum provides guided tours that offer in-depth insights into the exhibits and the stories behind the Nobel Peace Prize laureates. These tours are usually available at specific times, you can check the museum's website for the tour schedule and make any necessary reservations.

Temporary Exhibitions:

In addition to its permanent exhibitions, the Nobel Peace Center also hosts temporary exhibitions that highlight contemporary issues related to peace and conflict. These temporary exhibits offer a fresh perspective on current challenges and initiatives for peace.

Nobel Peace Prize Ceremony:

While the Nobel Peace Center is not the venue for the Nobel Peace Prize ceremony itself, it does host related events and activities during the Nobel Peace Prize week in December. If you happen to be in Oslo during this time, you may be able to witness some of the celebrations and exhibitions surrounding the prestigious award.

Visitor Facilities:

The Nobel Peace Center provides facilities such as a café, a gift shop, and restrooms for visitors. The café offers a selection of refreshments and light meals, making it a good spot to relax and reflect on your museum visit.

Nearby Attractions:

Since the Nobel Peace Center is centrally located, you can easily explore other attractions in Oslo after your visit. The City Hall, Aker Brygge waterfront, Royal Palace, and Akershus Fortress are all within walking distance.

Accessibility:

The Nobel Peace Center is designed to be accessible to all visitors. It provides wheelchair access, elevators, and accessible restrooms. Additionally, audio guides and exhibition texts are available in multiple languages.

Admission Fees:

There is an admission fee to enter the Nobel Peace Center, and the price may vary depending on age and discounts available. It's recommended to check the official website for the most accurate and up-to-date information on admission fees.

The New National Museum

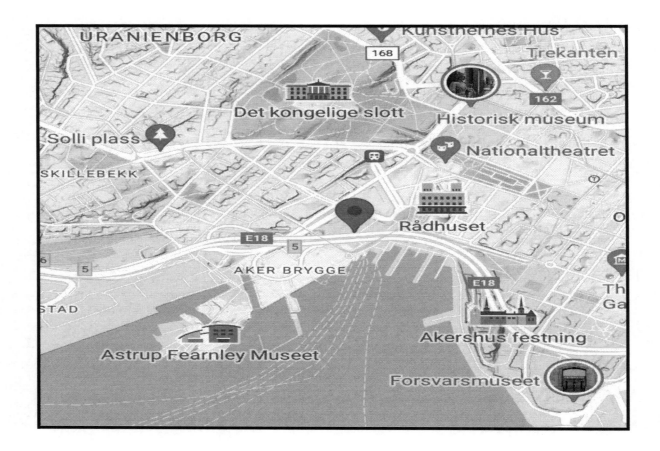

The new National Museum in Oslo, which took eight years to complete, is the largest museum in the Nordic countries. It opened on June 11, 2022, and it is a merger of three previous museums: the

National Gallery, the Museum of Contemporary Art, and the Norwegian Museum of Decorative Arts and Design.

The museum has a permanent exhibition of about 6,500 objects, which represent the history of art, architecture, and design in Norway from the Middle Ages to the present day. The exhibition is divided into four main themes:

- Early art and architecture
- The 19th century
- The 20th century
- The 21st century

The museum also has a number of temporary exhibitions, which showcase the work of Norwegian and international artists.

The new National Museum is located in Oslo, Norway, on Rådhusplassen (City Hall Square). It is a short walk from the Oslo Opera House and the Royal Palace.

Location:

The exact location is, Brynjulf Bulls plass 3, 0250 Oslo, Norway

Entry fee and Opening Hours:

It is open from Tuesday to Sunday, from 10:00am to 6:00pm. The museum remains closed on Mondays and public holidays. Admission fees are NOK 100 for adults, NOK 50 for students and seniors, and free for children under 18.

Note: Opening hours may vary on public holidays, so it's advisable to check the official beforehand.

With five floors, the museum is divided into four main sections:

1. The Collection Exhibition: This section displays the extensive collection of art, architecture, and design housed in the museum.
2. Temporary Exhibitions: This area hosts a variety of rotating exhibitions that change regularly.
3. The Munch Museum: Dedicated to the works of Edvard Munch, this section highlights the art of one of Norway's most famous artists.
4. The Architecture Gallery: Here, visitors can explore the rich history of architecture in Norway.

Highlights:

Edvard Munch's "The Scream": This iconic painting is a symbol of existential angst and one of the most famous artworks in the world. The National Gallery houses one version of "The Scream," "The Scream," created in 1893, was given as a donation to the National Gallery in 1910. Over time, it has gained a level of fame comparable to renowned works like Leonardo da Vinci's Mona Lisa (1503) and Van Gogh's Sunflowers (1888).

The impact of "The Scream" has been profound, inspiring filmmakers, cartoonists, and various other artists. It remains a powerful and enduring representation of human fear. The gallery showcases a diverse range of art styles and periods, making it a must-visit destination for art enthusiasts and culture lovers. It's definitely a must-see.

Norwegian Art:

The gallery offers a comprehensive collection of Norwegian art, spanning various periods and styles. From the romantic landscapes of Johan Christian Dahl to the vibrant works of Nikolai Astrup, you'll discover the richness and diversity of Norwegian artistic heritage.

International Art:

Alongside Norwegian art, the National Museum also features an impressive selection of international art. Explore masterpieces by artists like Claude Monet, Pablo Picasso, Vincent van Gogh, and many others.

Temporary Exhibitions:

The National Gallery hosts temporary exhibitions throughout the year, showcasing different themes, artists, or art movements. These exhibitions provide a fresh perspective and introduce visitors to new artistic experiences.

Facilities and Services:

Guided Tours: The gallery offers guided tours in multiple languages, providing insightful commentary on the artworks and their historical context. Check the website or inquire at the information desk for tour schedules.

Audio Guides:

Audio guides are available for rent, allowing visitors to explore the collection at their own pace. They provide detailed information about the artworks on display.

Café and Gift Shop:

The National Gallery has a café where you can relax, grab a bite to eat, and enjoy a cup of coffee. Additionally, there's a gift shop where you can find art-related souvenirs, books, and prints.

Accessibility:

The museum is wheelchair accessible, with ramps and elevators available. Accessible parking spaces and restrooms are also provided.

The MUNCH Museum

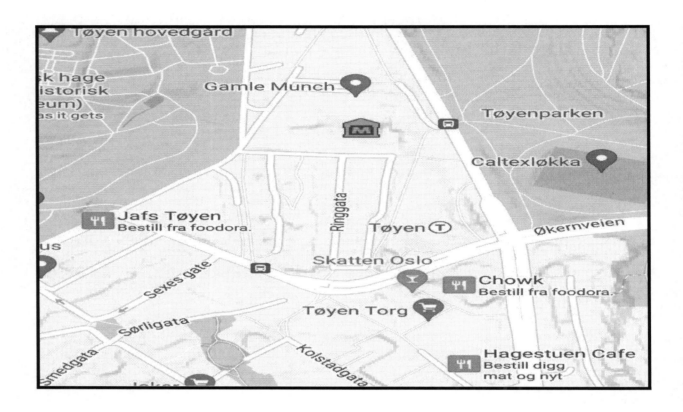

Location and Opening hours:

The MUNCH Museum is located in Bjørvika, Oslo, Norway. The address is Edvard Munch's plass 1, 0194 Oslo. The museum is open from 10:00 to 18:00 on Sundays, Tuesdays, and Wednesdays, and from 10:00 to 21:00 on Thursdays, Fridays, and Saturdays. The museum is closed on Mondays and on public holidays.

Opening hours for some specific dates:

- Christmas Eve: 10:00 to 14:00
- Christmas Day: 10:00 to 18:00
- Boxing Day: 10:00 to 18:00
- New Year's Eve: 10:00 to 14:00
- New Year's Day: 10:00 to 18:00

The museum is also closed on the following dates:

- 1 May (Labor Day)
- 17 May (Constitution Day)
- Ascension Day
- Whit Sunday
- Whit Monday

The New MUNCH museum in Oslo holds an extensive collection of art by the renowned artist Edvard Munch, gifted to the city of Oslo. It includes paintings, prints, and drawings, making it the largest collection of art by a single artist in the Nordic region. Munch is considered a pioneering figure in expressionism.

Alongside his works, the museum also exhibits world-class contemporary art on its 13 floors, with regularly changing exhibitions to offer new experiences to visitors. The museum hosts various artistic and cultural events throughout the year.

The museum building was designed by Spanish architect Juan Herreros and opened in October 2021. The museum houses over 28,000 works of art by Edvard Munch, including his most famous paintings, such as "The Scream", "The Dance of Life", and "Madonna".

The impressive museum building offers three dining options: Munch Deli & Café, Bistro Tolvte, and Kranen Bar. Additionally, visitors can explore the museum shop, which features gift items, products for children, literature about Munch, and other unique products inspired by his art.

To ensure admission, it is advisable to book timed tickets in advance, as the number of visitors per time slot is limited. If you have the Oslo Pass, you can obtain free tickets on-site during available time slots, but it is recommended to arrive early, as these tickets are limited and may require a short waiting period if they are fully reserved for the current time slot.

Visiting tips:

- Book your tickets in advance, especially if you are visiting during peak season.
- Allow plenty of time to explore the museum, as there is a lot to see.
- Wear comfortable shoes, as you will be doing a lot of walking.
- Take advantage of the museum's many educational resources, such as the audio guide and the children's activities.
- Be sure to visit the museum shop to pick up a souvenir of your visit.

Some of the most popular exhibits at the MUNCH museum:

- The Scream (1893): This painting is Munch's most famous work and is a powerful expression of anxiety and alienation.
- The Dance of Life (1909): This painting depicts a circle of dancers, representing the cycle of life and death.
- Madonna (1895): This painting is a portrait of Munch's sister, Inger, and is a symbol of love and compassion.
- The Frieze of Life (1893-1910): This series of paintings explores themes of love, loss, and death.
- The Starry Night (1909): This painting is a depiction of the night sky over Oslo and is one of Munch's most famous landscapes.

The Astrup Fearnley Museum of Modern

The Astrup Fearnley Museum of Modern Art is a renowned contemporary art museum located in Oslo, Norway. It features a diverse collection of international contemporary art, temporary exhibitions, and a striking architectural design. Here's a travel guide to help you make the most of your visit to the Astrup Fearnley Museum:

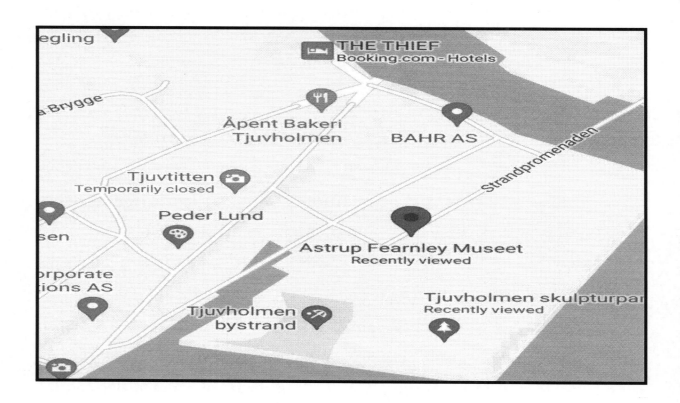

Location:

  The museum is situated in the Tjuvholmen neighborhood of Oslo, near Aker Brygge and the Oslo City Hall.

The address is Strandpromenaden 2, 0252 Oslo, Norway.

Admission Fees:

Adults: 160 NOK

Seniors (67+): 120 NOK

Students (18-26): 80 NOK

Children (0-17): Free

Oslo Pass: Free

Opening Hours:

Tuesday to Sunday: 11:00am to 5:00pm

Thursday: 11:00am to 7:00pm

Closed on Mondays

The museum is closed on public holidays.

Guided tours have a fee of 20 NOK.

Free admission is available on the last Thursday of every month.

Exhibitions and Collections:

The Astrup Fearnley Museum has an impressive collection of contemporary art, including works by renowned artists such as Damien Hirst, Jeff Koons, and Cindy Sherman. The museum showcases temporary exhibitions that change throughout the year.

Architecture:

The museum's building is a work of art in itself. Designed by renowned Italian architect Renzo Piano, it features a unique combination of wood, glass, and steel. Take some time to appreciate the building's striking exterior and its integration with the surrounding waterfront area.

Guided Tours and Audio Guides:

The museum offers guided tours that provide valuable insights into the artworks and exhibitions. If you prefer to explore the museum at your own pace, you can rent an audio guide that provides detailed explanations of the artworks and their significance.

Facilities and Amenities:

The museum has a café where you can grab a bite to eat or enjoy a cup of coffee while taking in the scenic views of the waterfront. There is also a museum shop where you can find unique art-related merchandise, books, and souvenirs to take home.

Ticket Information:

The museum charges an admission fee, with discounted rates for students, seniors, and children. Check their official website for the most up-to-date ticket prices.

It's worth noting that the Astrup Fearnley Museum of Modern Art offers free admission on the last Thursday of every month from 12:00 to 19:00. They also offer free admission to children under 20, members, and holders of the Oslo Pass

Nearby Attractions:

After visiting the Astrup Fearnley Museum, you can explore the Tjuvholmen neighborhood, which offers a vibrant mix of art galleries, restaurants, and shops.

A short walk away is Aker Brygge, a popular waterfront area known for its lively atmosphere, restaurants, and shopping opportunities.

If you have more time, you can also visit other notable attractions in Oslo, such as the Royal Palace, Vigeland Park, and the Oslo Opera House.

The Historical Museum

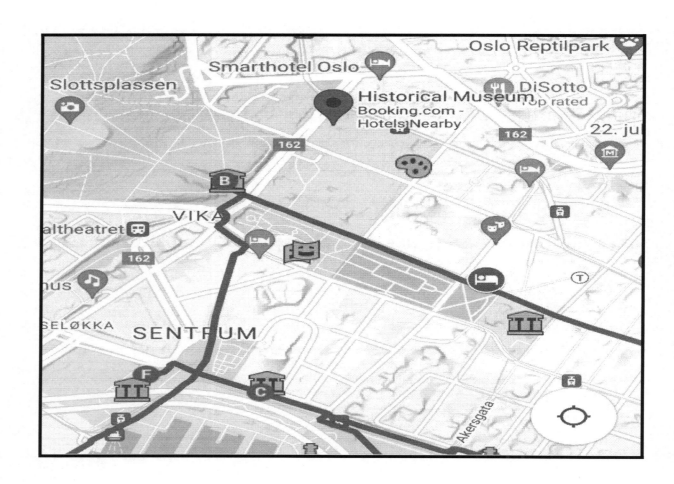

Location:

The Historical Museum is located at Frederiks gate 2, 0164 Oslo, Norway. It is situated in the city center, near the Royal Palace and within walking distance of other popular attractions.

Overview:

The largest museum of cultural history in Norway is the Historical Museum in Oslo. It boasts a vast collection of over one million objects that span from the Stone Age to the present day. The museum is divided into three main departments, each focusing on different aspects of history.

1. The Prehistoric and Medieval Collections department showcases artifacts from Norway's Stone Age, Bronze Age, Iron Age, and Viking Age. Notable highlights in this department include the Oseberg ship, Gokstad ship, and Tune ship.

2. The Ethnographic Collections department houses artifacts from various parts of the world, including Africa, Asia, the Americas, and Europe. Impressive exhibits in this department feature the Maori canoe from New Zealand, Chinese jade collection, and Tibetan Buddhist art collection.

3. The University History Collections department displays artifacts related to the history of the University of Oslo. Exhibits of interest in this department include the university's charter from 1811, professors' robes, and students' caps.

Among the museum's most popular exhibits are the Oseberg ship and Gokstad ship, both well-preserved Viking ships discovered in burial mounds. The Tune ship, although smaller, is also a remarkable sight. The museum also houses a collection of Egyptian mummies and funerary objects donated by the Egyptologist Christian Jürgensen

Thomsen. Additionally, there is a collection dedicated to the Sami people, showcasing their clothing, tools, and musical instruments.

Opening hours:

It is open every day from 10:00 to 16:00. Admission is free for children under 16, and adults pay 120 NOK

Tips to enjoy your tour of the museum:

Research and Plan:

- Before your visit, research the museum's website or other resources to learn about the museum's focus and the specific exhibits it offers.
- Check the museum's opening hours, ticket prices, and any special events or temporary exhibitions that may be happening during your visit.
- Note the museum's location and plan your transportation accordingly.

Arriving at the Museum:

- Allow yourself enough time to fully explore the museum without feeling rushed.

- Consider arriving early to avoid crowds, especially if it's a popular museum.
- Check if there are any guided tours available and if they align with your interests.

Museum Highlights:

- Ancient Civilizations: Discover artifacts from ancient Egypt, Greece, Rome, and other early civilizations. Marvel at intricate sculptures, pottery, jewelry, and mummies that offer a glimpse into the past.
- Medieval Era: Explore the medieval period with armor and weaponry displays, tapestries, and illuminated manuscripts. Learn about the feudal system, chivalry, and the rise of powerful empires.
- Renaissance and Enlightenment: Experience the cultural rebirth of Europe through paintings, sculptures, and scientific instruments from the Renaissance and Enlightenment periods. Admire works by renowned artists and philosophers.
- Industrial Revolution: Witness the transformation brought about by the Industrial Revolution with exhibits showcasing machinery, inventions, and models that revolutionized industries and daily life.
- World Wars: Understand the impact of World War I and II through photographs, personal accounts, military artifacts, and interactive displays. Gain insights into the socio-political changes that shaped the 20th century.

- Contemporary History: Engage with exhibitions dedicated to recent historical events, such as the Cold War, the Space Age, and significant social and political movements.

Museum Layout:

- Familiarize yourself with the museum's layout. This will help you plan your visit and ensure you don't miss any important exhibits.
- Some museums have multiple floors or wings, so prioritize the areas you're most interested in.

Engage with Exhibits:

- Take your time at each exhibit, reading the descriptions and studying the artifacts. Many museums provide audio guides or informational panels to enhance your understanding.
- Look for interactive displays that allow you to participate in the exhibits and get hands-on experiences.
- Pay attention to any special presentations or demonstrations that might be happening throughout the day.

Ask Questions:

If you have any questions or want more information about a particular exhibit, don't hesitate to ask the museum staff. They are usually knowledgeable and happy to assist you.

Take Breaks:

 Museums can be quite extensive, so don't forget to take breaks. Many museums have cafés or rest areas where you can relax and recharge before continuing your exploration.

Photography and Souvenirs:

- As of 2023, flash photography is prohibited in all areas of the museum, except for the conservation lab and storage areas. This is to protect the artifacts and exhibits from damage.

- Visit the museum shop or bookstore to browse through souvenirs, books, and replicas related to the exhibits. It's a great way to support the museum and take a piece of history home with you.

Reflect and Share:

- After your visit, take a moment to reflect on what you've learned and experienced.

- Share your experience with others through social media, a blog, or by simply discussing it with friends and family. It can be a great way to deepen your understanding and inspire others to visit the museum.

Guided Tours and Facilities:

The Historical Museum offers guided tours that provide in-depth information about the exhibits and the historical context behind them.

The Viking Planet

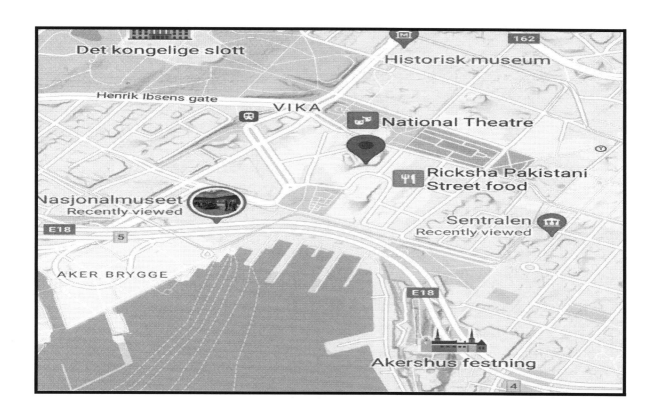

This is a digital museum in Oslo that uses VR technology, holograms, interactive screens, and 270-degree films to immerse visitors in the Viking Age.

Location:

The museum is located in the Tøyen neighborhood of Oslo, near the Natural History Museum. It was opened in 2019.

The Viking Planet offers a variety of experiences, including:

- A virtual reality tour of a Viking longship
- A hologram of a Viking warrior
- An interactive screen that allows visitors to learn about Viking weapons and armor
- A 270-degree film that takes visitors on a journey through Viking Norway
- A photo booth where visitors can take pictures of themselves in Viking costumes

The Viking Planet is open to the public from 10am to 6pm, Tuesday through Sunday. Admission is NOK 195 for adults, NOK 145 for children ages 6-16, and free for children under 6.

Here are some tips for visiting The Viking Planet:

- Allow plenty of time to explore the museum, as there is a lot to see and do.

- Wear comfortable shoes, as you will be doing a lot of walking.
- Take advantage of the interactive exhibits to learn more about the Viking Age.
- Be sure to watch the 270-degree film, which is a great way to experience Viking Norway.
- If you have children, be sure to take them to the photo booth to get their picture taken in Viking costumes.

Norwegian Museum of Cultural History

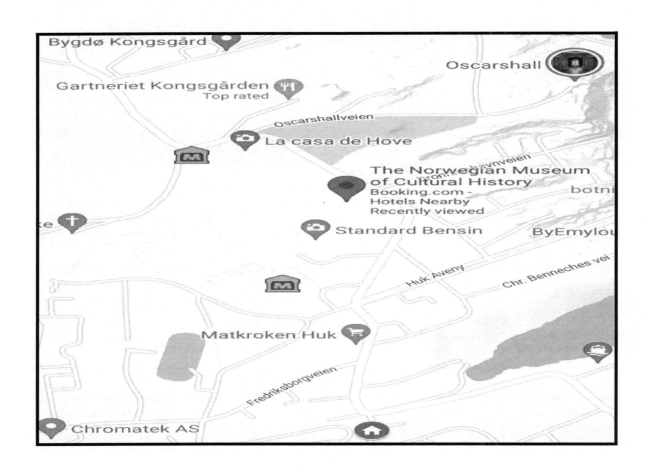

Overview:

The Norwegian Museum of Cultural History, also known as Norsk Folkemuseum. Established in 1894 by King Oscar II, it boasts a vast collection of over 150,000 artifacts from various regions of Norway. One of its main attractions is the expansive open-air museum, featuring more than 150 buildings that have been relocated from towns and rural areas across the country. These buildings span different historical periods, offering a glimpse into Norway's past.

The museum's primary objective is to preserve and showcase Norway's cultural heritage, which it accomplishes through exhibitions, educational programs, and research initiatives. As a popular tourist destination, it attracts more than 700,000 visitors annually.

Within the museum, visitors can explore the open-air museum, where they will encounter a diverse range of old buildings representing different eras. Additionally, the exhibition buildings house various collections, including folk costumes, household items, tools, and musical instruments. The museum also houses a library and archives containing extensive information about Norwegian cultural history, as well as a dedicated research center conducting studies on the subject.

Overall, the Norwegian Museum of Cultural History offers a captivating and enriching experience for individuals of all ages, providing valuable insights into Norway's history and culture.

Location:

Address: P. O. Engergate 1, 0258 Oslo, Norway.

Opening hours and entry fee:

The museum is open from 10:00am to 5:00pm, Tuesday to Sunday. Admission fees are NOK 100 for adults, NOK 50 for students and seniors, and free for children under 18.

Highlights of the Museum:

- Open-Air Exhibits: The museum features over 160 historic buildings from different regions of Norway. You can explore traditional farmhouses, stave churches, and other structures, providing a glimpse into Norway's architectural history.

- The Gol Stave Church: This iconic stave church dates back to the 13th century and is one of the museum's most treasured artifacts.

- Sami Culture: The museum has exhibits dedicated to the indigenous Sami people, showcasing their traditional costumes, crafts, and way of life.

- Folklore and Folk Art: Discover Norwegian folk traditions, such as traditional costumes, woodcarving, rosemaling (decorative painting), and traditional music.

Indoor Exhibits:

- The Main Building: Explore the extensive collection of artifacts, including traditional clothing, silverware, and historical artifacts from various periods of Norwegian history.

- The Toy Museum: Located in the Main Building, this museum displays a fascinating collection of toys from different eras, providing insights into Norwegian childhoods.

- Temporary Exhibitions: The museum hosts rotating exhibitions on various topics related to Norwegian culture and history.

Practical Tips:

- Plan Sufficient Time: The museum is vast, and there is much to see. Allocate at least 2-3 hours for your visit.
- Comfortable Clothing: As it is an open-air museum, be prepared for outdoor walking and dress accordingly, especially during colder seasons.
- Guided Tours: The museum offers guided tours in several languages, providing in-depth information and insights. Check the schedule on their website or inquire at the information desk.
- Facilities: The museum has a café and a museum shop where you can grab refreshments or purchase souvenirs.

Additional Information:

- Entrance Fees: The museum charges an admission fee, and prices may vary depending on age and season. Check the museum's website for the current rates.
- Guided Tours: The museum offers guided tours in English, Norwegian, and other languages. If you prefer a more in-depth experience, consider joining one of these tours.
- Photography: You are generally allowed to take photographs for personal use, but some indoor exhibitions may have restrictions. Make sure to respect any signage regarding photography.

The Natural History Museum

The Natural History Museum in Oslo is Norway's largest and oldest museum of natural history. It is located in the Tøyen neighborhood of Oslo, near the Botanical Garden.

- The museum was founded in 1812 and houses a collection of over 6 million objects, including fossils, plants, animals, and minerals.

- The museum has four permanent exhibitions:
    - The Earth: This exhibition explores the geological history of Earth, from its formation to the present day.
    - Life: This exhibition explores the diversity of life on Earth, from the smallest microbes to the largest dinosaurs.
    - People: This exhibition explores the relationship between humans and the natural world.
    - Climate House: This exhibition explores the impact of climate change on the natural world.
- The museum also offers a variety of temporary exhibitions, educational programs, and events.

The Natural History Museum is open to the public from 10am to 5pm, Tuesday through Sunday. Admission is free for children under the age of 16.

- Tips for visiting the Natural History Museum:
- Allow plenty of time to explore the museum, as there is a lot to see and do.
- Wear comfortable shoes, as you will be doing a lot of walking.
- Take advantage of the interactive exhibits to learn more about the natural world.
- Be sure to visit the Climate House to learn about the impact of climate change.
- If you have children, be sure to check out the museum's educational programs and events.

The New Climate House in Oslo:

- The Climate House is an exhibition space located in the Natural History Museum in Oslo.
- The exhibition open in 2020 and is designed to educate visitors about climate change.
- The exhibition features a variety of interactive exhibits, such as a virtual reality experience that allows visitors to explore a world three degrees Celsius hotter.
- The Climate House also offers a variety of educational programs, such as workshops and lectures.

The Climate House is open to the public from 10am to 5pm, Tuesday through Sunday. Admission is free.

Tips for visiting the Climate House:

- Allow plenty of time to explore the exhibition, as there is a lot to see and do.
- Wear comfortable shoes, as you will be doing a lot of walking.
- Take advantage of the interactive exhibits to learn more about climate change.
- Be sure to attend one of the educational programs offered by the Climate House.

Other art galleries in Oslo

- Kunstnernes Hus is a notable gallery in Oslo known for its contemporary art and historical significance.

- Blaafarveværket, located an hour from Oslo, is a unique museum combining art, culture, and outdoor activities.

- Ramme is an art gallery and farm that follows the footsteps of the renowned artist Edvard Munch, just 40 minutes from Oslo.

- Henie Onstad Kunstsenter, situated on the Høvikodden peninsula, is a museum specializing in modern and contemporary art.

- Fineart Oslo is Norway's largest gallery, featuring prints, photographs, paintings, drawings, and various other art forms.

- Kunsthall Oslo is a non-profit art space focusing on international contemporary art and new commissions.

- Gerhardsen Gerner Oslo is a gallery showcasing works by high-profile contemporary artists from Norway and around the world.

- The Mini Bottle Gallery is a unique attraction housing the world's largest collection of miniature bottles.

- QB Gallery, established in 2014, focuses on contemporary art, primarily from Norwegian artists.

- Format Oslo is a leading Norwegian craft intermediary with temporary exhibitions of Norwegian and international artists.

- Galleri Dobloug exhibits international art and separate exhibitions by Norwegian painters and sculptors.

- Gallery Albin Upp is an art gallery and café located in an authentic farmer's house from the 19th century.

- Purenkel is a gallery at Grünerløkka with an exciting range of visual arts, crafts, sculpture, and design from Norwegian artists.
- Galleri Mini mainly exhibits art by young artists in Gamlebyen, established by artist Cecilia Kristensen.
- Galleri ROM art + architecture is an independent organization promoting art and architecture through exhibitions, lectures, and public art displays.
- Blomqvist Auction House Gallery is Norway's largest art shop and auction house, established in 1870.
- TBS Gallery is a cultural center dedicated to the artist Tore Bjørn Skjølsvik, featuring a gallery and museum.
- Fotogalleriet is Oslo's only gallery devoted to camera-based art, showcasing Norwegian artists' work.
- Galleri Brandstrup is a contemporary art gallery that exhibits both well-established artists and young talents, with a focus on Nordic contemporary art.
- Soft galleri: Norwegian Textile Artists is a gallery exhibiting the work of members of the Norwegian Textile Artists group.
- Young Artists' Society runs an art gallery as an exhibition space for international and Norwegian artists.
- Pushwagner Gallery, located at Tjuvholmen, features the work of the late artist Hariton Pushwagner.
- Galleri Heer is a contemporary art gallery with a diverse range of artists, including both young and old, male and female, and debutantes.
- ISCA Gallery is an independent contemporary art gallery dedicated to promoting and exhibiting Norwegian artists.
- Golsa is a contemporary art gallery located at Solli Plass.

- Peder Lund is an art gallery at Tjuvholmen, featuring international modern and contemporary art as well as young contemporary artists.

Chapter 8:

Outdoor Activities in Oslo

Bygdøy Peninsula

Bygdøy Peninsula is a beautiful and historic area located in Oslo, Norway. Known for its museums, beaches, and recreational areas, Bygdøy is a popular destination for both locals and tourists.

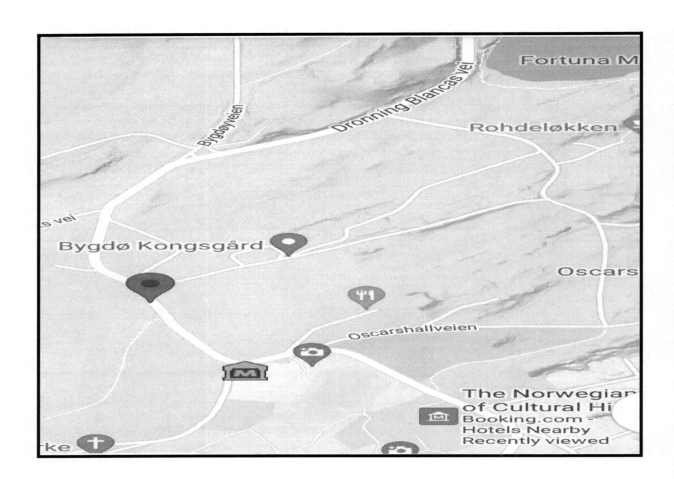

Getting There:

Bygdøy Peninsula is easily accessible from central Oslo. You can take a ferry from the City Hall (Rådhusbrygge 3) to Bygdøy, which offers a scenic and enjoyable ride. Alternatively, you can take bus number 30 from the city center, which will take you directly to Bygdøy.

Museums:

Bygdøy is home to several world-class museums, making it a haven for history and culture enthusiasts. The most famous museum on the peninsula is the Viking Ship Museum, which houses well-preserved Viking ships and artifacts. The Kon-Tiki Museum, dedicated to the famous explorer Thor Heyerdahl, showcases his expeditions and the vessels he used. Additionally, the Fram Museum focuses on polar exploration, featuring the ship Fram used by Fridtjof Nansen and Roald Amundsen. Other notable museums include the Norwegian Folk Museum, showcasing traditional Norwegian life, and the Holocaust Center, documenting the Holocaust and promoting human rights.

Beaches and Outdoor Activities:

Bygdøy Peninsula offers some lovely beaches where you can relax and soak up the sun during the summer months. Huk Beach is the most popular beach in the area, offering a sandy shoreline, swimming areas, and even a nudist section. Paradisbukta and Bygdøy Sjøbad are also great options for beachgoers. If you're into outdoor activities, you can rent bikes or kayaks to explore the peninsula's beautiful coastline and nature trails.

Royal Estate:

Bygdøy is also home to the Royal Estate, which consists of several buildings, including Oscarshall, a beautiful neoclassical castle built in the 19th century. Although the estate is not open to the public, you can still admire its stunning architecture and stroll through the surrounding gardens.

Bygdøy Farm:

If you're traveling with kids or simply enjoy farm animals, a visit to Bygdøy Farm is a must. This charming farm offers pony rides, feeding opportunities, and a chance to interact with various farm animals, including sheep, goats, pigs, and chickens.

Restaurants and Cafés:

Bygdøy has a range of dining options to suit different tastes. Whether you're looking for traditional Norwegian cuisine, international flavors, or a quick snack, you'll find something to satisfy your cravings. The area also has a few cozy cafés where you can enjoy a cup of coffee and some Norwegian pastries.

Bygdøy Forest:

To escape the hustle and bustle of the city, take a walk or go for a jog in the serene Bygdøy Forest. This vast green space offers numerous trails, perfect for nature lovers and outdoor enthusiasts.

Holmenkollen Ski Museum and Jump

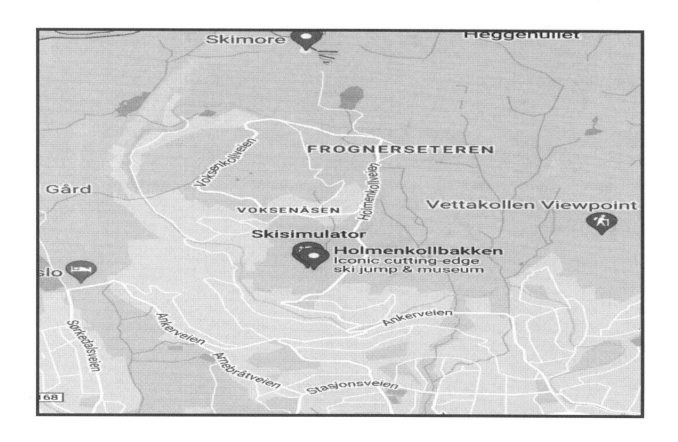

The Holmenkollen Ski Museum and Jump is a popular tourist attraction located in Oslo, Norway. It is the oldest ski museum in the world and offers visitors a unique opportunity to explore the history of skiing while enjoying breathtaking views of the city.

Holmenkollen Ski Museum and Jump Oslo

Getting there:

The museum is situated in the Holmenkollen neighborhood, approximately 10 kilometers northwest of central Oslo. You can reach the museum by public transportation, specifically by taking the T-bane (metro) line 1 to the Holmenkollen station. From there, it's a short walk to the museum. The exact address is Kongeveien 5, 0787 Oslo, Norway.

Holmenkollen Ski Jump:

The ski jump is a remarkable architectural structure and an iconic symbol of Oslo. It has been used for various ski competitions, including the Winter Olympics. Visitors can take an elevator to the top of the jump for panoramic views of Oslo and the surrounding fjords. If you're feeling adventurous, you can even try the zipline that takes you down from the top of the jump.

Ski Museum:

The museum provides a fascinating journey through the history of skiing. Exhibits showcase antique skis, equipment, and memorabilia, highlighting the development of skiing over the centuries. You'll also find displays on famous Norwegian skiers and the evolution of ski technology. Interactive exhibits and multimedia presentations make the experience engaging for visitors of all ages.

Virtual Reality Experience:

For an immersive experience, the museum offers a virtual reality ski simulator. Strap on the virtual reality goggles and experience the thrill of skiing down famous Norwegian slopes.

Ski Simulator:

Adjacent to the museum, you'll find a ski simulator where you can try your hand at a virtual ski jump. Test your skills and see if you can land a perfect jump.

Holmenkollen Zipline (New):

Experience the thrill of zipping down the renowned Holmenkollen Ski Jump, descending all the way to the hill's base! The Kollensvevet zipline offers an exhilarating 361-meter ride filled with pure adrenaline. As you glide down from this iconic landmark, you'll be treated to an unforgettable panoramic view of Oslo.

Cafes and Restaurants:

After exploring the museum and ski jump, you can relax and enjoy a meal or a hot drink at one of the onsite cafes and restaurants. They offer a range of Norwegian and international cuisine, and many have panoramic views of Oslo.

Souvenir Shop:

Don't forget to visit the museum's souvenir shop, where you can purchase skiing-related memorabilia, traditional Norwegian clothing, and other unique items.

Outdoor Activities:

Holmenkollen is surrounded by beautiful nature, offering opportunities for outdoor activities such as hiking, skiing, and sledding. You can explore the nearby trails and enjoy the picturesque scenery.

Opening Hours and Admission:

The museum is typically open from 10 am to 4 pm, although the hours may vary seasonally. Admission fees apply, and discounted tickets are available for children, students, and seniors.

Nordmarka Forest:

It is located about 30 kilometers (19 miles) northwest of the city center. It offers a wonderful escape from the hustle and bustle of urban life, with stunning scenery, tranquil lakes, and numerous outdoor activities. Here's a travel guide to help you explore Nordmarka Forest:

Getting There:

- By Public Transport: Take the subway (T-bane) line 1 to Frognerseteren or Sognsvann stations, both located at the edge of Nordmarka Forest. You can also take bus number 54 or 550 to Sognsvann.
- By Car: If you prefer to drive, you can reach Nordmarka Forest by following the signs to Sognsvann or Frognerseteren. There are parking areas available at both locations.

Hiking and Trails:

- Sognsvann: This is a popular starting point for many hiking trails in Nordmarka. The circular trail around the picturesque Sognsvann Lake is an easy and enjoyable hike suitable for all ages.
- Frognerseteren: From Frognerseteren, you can access several trails that lead deeper into the forest. Try the hike to Ullevålseter, a cozy cabin with a café where you can take a break and enjoy traditional Norwegian food.

Skiing and Winter Activities:

- Nordmarka is a winter wonderland, offering excellent opportunities for cross-country skiing. The trails are well-maintained, and you can rent ski equipment in Oslo if needed.

- Frognerseteren to Tryvann: This popular ski route takes you from Frognerseteren to Tryvann Winter Park, offering beautiful views of Oslo along the way.

Lakes and Picnic Spots:

- Nøklevann: Located in the southern part of Nordmarka, Nøklevann is a serene lake surrounded by forests. It's a great spot for a picnic or a leisurely stroll.
- Maridalsvannet: This is Oslo's largest lake and a popular destination for swimming, fishing, and kayaking during the summer months.

Wildlife and Nature:

Nordmarka Forest is home to various wildlife, including deer, foxes, and a wide range of bird species. Keep your eyes open and be respectful of their habitats. In late summer and autumn, you can also forage for wild berries and mushrooms, but make sure you have the necessary knowledge and permits.

Safety Tips:

- Dress appropriately for the weather and wear comfortable shoes for hiking.
- Bring sufficient water and snacks, especially if you plan on spending a significant amount of time in the forest.
- Follow the marked trails and pay attention to any warning signs or advice from local authorities.
- Be cautious with open fires and adhere to any fire restrictions that may be in place.

- Remember to respect nature and leave no trace behind to preserve the beauty of Nordmarka Forest for future visitors.

Oslo Botanical Garden

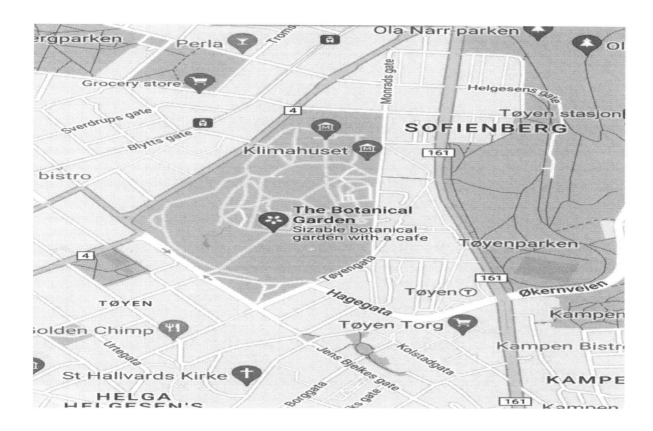

Location:

The Oslo Botanical Garden is located in the Tøyen neighborhood of Oslo, Norway. The official address of the museum is Sars' gate 1, 0562 Oslo, Norway.

Opening hours :

- April – September: 10:00 AM to 6:00 PM
- October – March: 10:00 AM to 3:00 PM

The last entry is 30 minutes before closing.

Highlights and Attractions:

- Greenhouses: Explore the various greenhouses that house a diverse range of plant species, including tropical plants, cacti, and orchids. The Palm House is particularly impressive.
- Outdoor Gardens: Take a leisurely stroll through the outdoor gardens, featuring beautifully landscaped areas, ponds, and a rock garden. Don't miss the alpine garden, herb garden, and rose garden.
- Arboretum: Discover a wide variety of trees from around the world in the arboretum. It's a peaceful and serene area for nature enthusiasts.

Botanical Museum

Events and Activities:

- Guided Tours: Take part in the tours led by the garden staff to learn more about the significance of the plant collections and to develop a deeper understanding of them.
- Workshops & Lectures: Keep a watch on the garden's calendar of events for information about workshops, lectures, and special

events pertaining to gardening, botany, and environmental preservation.

- Picnics: Take a picnic and take in the tranquil setting. The garden has specific picnic places where you can unwind and rest.
- Photography: The garden has fantastic opportunities for photography aficionados with its beautiful scenery and vibrant plant life.

Useful tips

- Admission: Although the garden is often free to enter, donations are welcome to help with its upkeep and development.
- Weather and Attire: Before your visit, check the weather forecast and dress appropriately. Because you'll be walking a lot, choose comfy shoes.
- Amenities: There are drinking fountains and restrooms in the garden. There may also be a tiny café or kiosk where you may get refreshments, but it's best to bring your own food and water.
- The garden is normally accessible, but some spots could have uneven walkways. There are wheelchair-accessible spaces and resting spots scattered around the garden.
- During your stay, keep in mind to respect the environment and the flora.

Sognsvann Lake

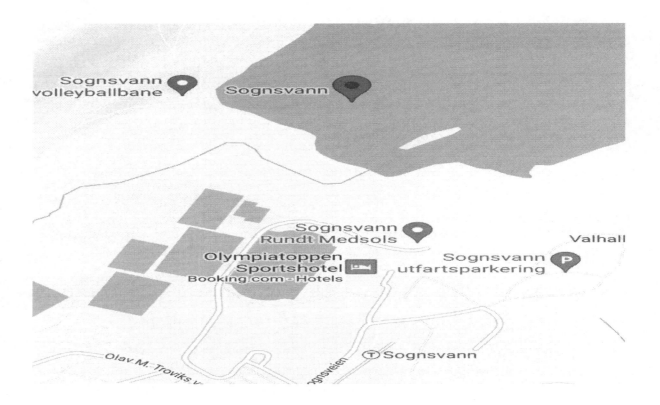

Sognsvann Lake is a popular recreational area located just outside Oslo, Norway. It is known for its beautiful surroundings, peaceful atmosphere, and opportunities for outdoor activities.

Location and Access:

Sognsvann Lake is situated in the Nordmarka forest, approximately 20 minutes north of central Oslo. The exact address is; *Sognsvann lake, 0890 Oslo, Norway.* The lake is easily accessible by public transportation. Take the T-bane (metro) line 3 to the Sognsvann station, which is the final stop on this line.

Hiking and Walking:

Sognsvann is a fantastic destination for hiking and walking enthusiasts. The area offers several well-marked trails of varying difficulty levels. The most popular is the 3.3-kilometer loop around the lake, which is relatively easy and suitable for all fitness levels. You can also explore the surrounding forest and venture onto longer trails that connect to Nordmarka's extensive trail network.

Swimming and Beach:

During the summer months, Sognsvann Lake is a great spot for swimming and sunbathing. The water is generally clean and refreshing. There is a sandy beach area where you can relax, have a picnic, or enjoy a barbecue. Keep in mind that the water can be cold, so swimming might be more enjoyable on warmer days.

Winter Activities:

Sognsvann transforms into a winter wonderland during the colder months. Cross-country skiing is a popular activity in the area, and there are several well-groomed trails for both beginners and experienced skiers. You can rent skis from nearby sports shops if you don't have your own equipment. Additionally, some sections of the lake may freeze over, allowing for ice skating.

Amenities and Facilities:

Sognsvann has facilities to ensure visitors' comfort and convenience. There are public toilets, changing rooms, and showers available near the lake. You'll also find picnic tables and benches where you can relax and enjoy a meal or snacks. Don't forget to pack your own food and drinks, as there are no restaurants or shops in the immediate vicinity.

Nature and Wildlife:

Sognsvann is surrounded by lush forests and provides a peaceful retreat from the bustling city. The area is home to a variety of wildlife, including birds, squirrels, and occasionally deer. Birdwatching enthusiasts can spot several species throughout the year. Respect the environment and not disturb the wildlife.

Safety and Considerations:

While Sognsvann is generally safe, it's essential to take precautions when enjoying outdoor activities. Stay on marked trails, especially if you're unfamiliar with the area. Make sure to dress appropriately for the weather and wear sturdy shoes for hiking. During the winter, be aware of ice conditions and always follow safety guidelines for ice skating and skiing.

Photography Opportunities:

Sognsvann's natural beauty provides excellent opportunities for photography. Whether you're capturing the serene lake, vibrant autumn colors, or winter landscapes, be sure to bring your camera or smartphone to capture the memories.

Hiking and biking trails

1. Nordmarka:

Popular trails in Nordmarka include Sognsvann Lake to Ullevålseter, Frognerseteren to Tryvannstua, and Skar to Skjennungen. You can also visit historical sites like the old abandoned Tryvann Tower and the iconic Frognerseteren Café.

2. Bygdøy Peninsula:

The coastal trail around Bygdøy offers beautiful views of the Oslo Fjord and passes by beaches and charming residential areas. You can combine your hike or bike ride with visits to popular museums like the Viking Ship Museum, Fram Museum, and the Kon-Tiki Museum.

3. Østmarka:

Østmarka is an expansive woodland located east of Oslo and offers a tranquil setting for hiking and biking. Trails like Løkka-Grønmo and Haukåsen-Skulerud are popular among outdoor enthusiasts. The area is also dotted with beautiful lakes, including Nøklevann and Østensjøvannet, where you can enjoy a refreshing swim or a picnic.

Lysakerelven River:

The Lysakerelven River runs from Maridalsvannet Lake to the Oslo Fjord, providing a picturesque route for hikers and cyclists. The trail follows the river and passes through lush greenery, charming neighborhoods, and historic sites. You can start your journey from the idyllic Sognsvann Lake and make your way down to the fjord.

Grefsenkollen:

Grefsenkollen is a popular recreational area located north of the city center, offering stunning views of Oslo and the surrounding areas. The trail to Grefsenkollen is relatively short but provides a rewarding experience, especially during sunset. At the top, you'll find Grefsenkollen Restaurant, where you can enjoy a meal or a refreshing beverage while taking in the panoramic views.

Tips for Hiking and Biking in Oslo:

- Check the weather forecast before heading out and dress appropriately for the conditions.
- Pack essentials such as water, snacks, a map or GPS, sunscreen, and insect repellent.
- Respect the environment and follow Leave No Trace principles.
- Make sure to have a sturdy bike or rent one from various bike rental shops in the city.
- Consider joining guided tours or group activities to enhance your experience and meet fellow outdoor enthusiasts.
- Remember to always prioritize safety and follow any rules or regulations specific to each trail. Enjoy your hiking and biking adventures in Oslo!

Boat Tours and Kayaking

1. Oslo Fjord Boat Tours:

There are various operators offering guided tours that take you around the fjord, providing breathtaking views of the city's coastline and nearby islands. You can choose from different types of tours, including sightseeing cruises, sunset tours, or even dinner cruises.

2. Kayaking in Oslo Fjord:

If you prefer a more active experience, you can rent a kayak and explore the Oslo Fjord at your own pace. Several companies in Oslo offer kayak rentals, including single and double kayaks, as well as guided kayak tours. Paddling through the fjord gives you a unique perspective of the city and allows you to discover hidden coves and small islands.

3. Guided City Sightseeing by Boat:

Take a guided boat tour through the city's canals and waterways to explore Oslo's landmarks and attractions. These tours often pass through the inner parts of Oslo, offering views of iconic sites like the Oslo Opera House, Akershus Fortress, and the modern waterfront developments. It's a relaxing way to see the city from a different angle.

4. Oslo Hop-On Hop-Off Boat:

Similar to the popular hop-on hop-off buses, Oslo also has a hop-on hop-off boat service. This allows you to explore the city at your own pace, hopping on and off the boat at various stops along the way. You can combine this with other forms of transportation to create a comprehensive sightseeing experience.

5. Oslo River Cruises:

Experience Oslo from the perspective of its rivers. There are river cruises available on the Akerselva River, which runs through the city center. These cruises offer a unique way to see Oslo's vibrant neighborhoods, picturesque parks, and historical buildings along the riverbanks.

Before embarking on any boat tour or kayaking activity, check the availability, schedules, and safety guidelines provided by the tour operators and dress appropriately for your chosen activity.

Skiing and snowboarding

Due to its proximity to various ski resorts and beautiful winter landscapes, Oslo is a popular destination for winter sports lovers.

1. Best Time to Visit:

The ski season in Oslo typically runs from late November to April, with the peak season being December to February. During this time, you can expect good snow conditions and well-groomed slopes.

2. Ski Resorts near Oslo:

Here are some popular options:

- Oslo Winter Park (Tryvann): Located just 30 minutes from the city center. It offers a variety of slopes, including beginner-friendly runs and more challenging terrain for experienced skiers and snowboarders.

- Norefjell Ski Resort: Situated about 2 hours from Oslo, Norefjell is one of Norway's largest ski resorts. It has a good selection of slopes, with options for all skill levels. The resort also offers cross-country skiing trails and a terrain park.

- Hemsedal Ski Resort: Although a bit farther from Oslo (around 3 hours), Hemsedal is worth the trip for its extensive ski area. It has a wide range of slopes and excellent off-piste opportunities for advanced skiers and snowboarders.

- Kongsberg Skisenter: Located about 1.5 hours from Oslo, Kongsberg Skisenter is a smaller resort with family-friendly slopes and a terrain park. It's a good option if you're looking for a quieter skiing experience.

3. Equipment Rental and Lessons:

If you don't have your own skiing or snowboarding equipment, you can rent them at the ski resorts or in Oslo city center. Most resorts have rental shops where you can find a wide selection of gear. However, many resorts offer ski and snowboard lessons for beginners or those looking to improve their skills. Book lessons in advance, especially during peak season.

4. Transportation:

To reach the ski resorts from Oslo, you can use public transportation or rent a car. Several resorts offer bus services from Oslo to the slopes, making it convenient for visitors. Alternatively, you can rent a car and drive to the resorts, which gives you more flexibility in terms of schedules and exploring nearby areas.

5. Other Winter Activities:

In addition to skiing and snowboarding, you can try ice skating at Frogner Stadium or Spikersuppa Ice Rink in the city center. Cross-country skiing is also popular in Oslo, with many well-maintained trails available in nearby forests and parks. If you're interested in winter sports, but not skiing or snowboarding, you can try tobogganing or snowshoeing.

6. Safety Precautions:

When participating in any winter sport, it's important to prioritize safety. Make sure to wear appropriate clothing, including warm and waterproof layers, and always wear a helmet when skiing or snowboarding. Follow the rules and guidelines of the ski resorts, and be aware of your own skill level to avoid accidents or injuries.

Chapter 9

<u>Dining and nightlife in Oslo</u>

(Local recommendations)

Traditional Norwegian cuisine in Oslo offers a taste of the country's rich culinary heritage. These typical Norwegian dishes can be found in a variety of Norwegian-themed restaurants and diners in Oslo.

Traditional Norwegian dishes you can try in Oslo:

1. Fårikål: This is Norway's national dish and consists of slow-cooked lamb and cabbage. It is typically seasoned with salt, pepper, and whole black peppercorns. Fårikål is traditionally enjoyed during the autumn months.

Fårikål

2. Lutefisk: This dish is made from dried whitefish, typically cod, soaked in lye for several days to rehydrate and soften it. It is then cooked and served with boiled potatoes, peas, bacon, and mustard sauce.

3. Rømmegrøt: Rømmegrøt is a creamy sour cream porridge made with flour, butter, and sour cream. It is often served with cured meats and flatbread.

Lutefisk

Rømmegrøt

4. **Rakfisk:** Rakfisk is fermented fish, usually trout or char, which is cured in salt and spices for several months. It is often served with flatbread, sour cream, red onions, and potatoes.

Rakfisk

5. **Raspeballer:** Also known as boller, this is a type of potato dumpling filled with salted and dried codfish. It is served with bacon, sausage, and butter sauce.

Raspeballer

6. Krumkake: A popular Norwegian dessert, krumkake is a thin, crisp waffle-like cookie made from flour, butter, sugar, and cream. It is often rolled into a cone shape and filled with whipped cream.

Krumkake

7. Riskrem: This is a traditional rice pudding dessert often served during Christmas. It is made with rice, sugar, vanilla, and whipped cream, and topped with a red berry sauce.

Riskrem

8. Smalahove: This is a traditional dish from Western Norway that consists of a sheep's head, usually boiled or steamed, and served with potatoes, rutabaga, and mashed peas.

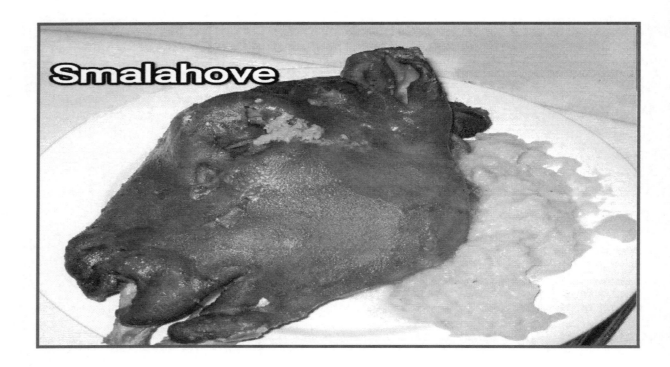

Smalahove

9. Kjøttkaker: These are large meatballs made with ground beef, pork, and breadcrumbs. They are typically served with brown sauce, potatoes, and lingonberries.

10. Pinnekjøtt: This is a dish of lamb ribs that are salted, dried, and then steamed. It is typically served with potatoes, cabbage, and mustard.

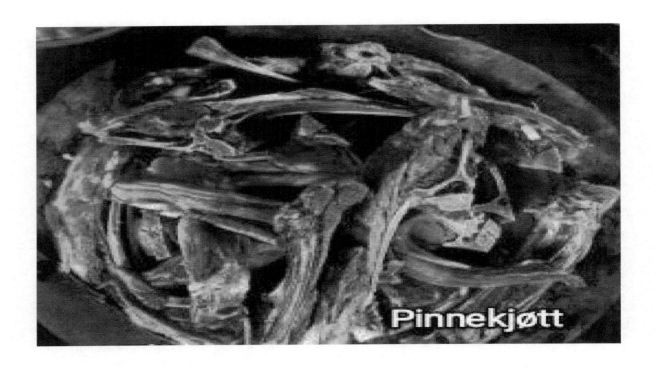

Pinnekjøtt

11. Vafler: These are waffles that are typically served with jam, whipped cream, or ice cream. They are a popular dessert or snack in Norway.

Vafler

Traditional Norwegian cuisine establishments in Oslo:

1. Stortorvets Gjæstgiveri is located at Grensen 1, 0159 Oslo, Norway. It is a traditional Norwegian eatery situated in an 18th-century structure. They offer a range of Norwegian delicacies, including reindeer, moose, and lutefisk.

2. Gamle Raadhus Restaurant is located at Nedre Slottsgate 1, 0157 Oslo, Norway. It is a Michelin-approved establishment that specializes in seasonal Norwegian cuisine. It boasts a charming ambiance within a 17th-century building.

3. Kaffistova is located at Karl Johans gate 31, 0154 Oslo. It is a beloved Norwegian café with a rich history dating back to 1900. They are renowned for their smørbrød, or open-faced sandwiches, featuring classic Norwegian flavors.

4. Rorbua is located at Stranden 71, 0150 Oslo, Norway. It is a restaurant located in an authentic Norwegian fisherman's cabin known as a rorbu. Their menu showcases delectable seafood options such as fish soup and grilled salmon.

5. Fiskerietis is located at Youngstorget 3, 0181 Oslo. It is a seafood restaurant situated in the Aker Brygge district. They offer an

extensive selection of fresh seafood dishes, including lobster, crab, and shrimp.

6. Larsen Restaurant is located at Bogstadveien 27, 0366 Oslo. It is a Michelin-approved eatery that serves innovative Norwegian cuisine. They prioritize seasonal ingredients and emphasize sustainability in their culinary creations.

7. Dovrehallen is located at Storgata 22, 0184 Oslo. It is a traditional Norwegian restaurant that has been serving up hearty food since 1863. The menu features dishes like reindeer stew, lamb chops, and salmon.

8. Restaurant Schrøder: Tucked away in the Grünerløkka district at Waldemar Thranes gate 8, 0171 Oslo, Restaurant Schrøder is a local favorite for experiencing authentic Norwegian fare. This cozy establishment specializes in traditional homemade dishes like (potato dumplings), lapskaus (meat and vegetable stew), and rømmegrøt.

The Salmon

The food scene in Oslo has undergone a remarkable shift, transitioning from overpriced and bland to a vibrant and playful experience. From fine dining to street food courts, there's something to suit every taste.

Location:

Strandpromenaden 11 0254 Oslo

The Salmon is a new restaurant and educational establishment located on Tjuvholmen, in the harbor of Oslo. It is dedicated to promoting knowledge about Norwegian salmon farming and showcasing Norwegian salmon as a product. The restaurant offers a variety of salmon dishes prepared in both traditional and modern styles.

One of the unique features of The Salmon is its own smokehouse, where they smoke fresh fish and also sell traditional Gravlax, a Nordic specialty. Visitors can enjoy learning about salmon while savoring delicious dishes in a central location in Oslo.

Duckpin

This is a new restaurant located in the heart of Oslo, precisely in Torggata.

Location:

The exact location is Torggata 28 0183 Oslo

Duckpin offers a unique dining and bowling experience. In addition to savoring delicious American cuisine, patrons can delight in the thrilling fusion of dining and bowling, creating the perfect destination for enjoying meals and bowling without the requirement of traditional bowling shoes, thanks to the use of smaller balls.

International restaurants in oslo

International restaurants in Oslo along with their locations and the types of cuisine they serve:

- Italian Restaurants: Located at Stortingsgata 22, Eataly offers a variety of Italian dishes such as pasta, pizza, and gelato.
- Hanami: Situated at Bygdøy Allé 62, Hanami offers traditional Japanese cuisine including sushi, sashimi, and tempura.
- Jaipur: Located at Tordenskiolds gate 12, Jaipur serves Indian dishes with a focus on North Indian cuisine.
- Spice India: Situated at Møllergata 37, Spice India offers a variety of Indian curries, tandoori dishes, and biryanis.
- Eik Annen Etage: Located at Rosteds gate 15, Eik Annen Etage serves Thai and Asian fusion cuisine.
- Bangkok Thai: Situated at Skippergata 32, Bangkok Thai offers a range of Thai dishes with vegetarian and vegan options.
- Beirut Restaurant: Located at Storgata 28, Beirut Restaurant specializes in Lebanese and Middle Eastern cuisine.
- Munchies Falafel: Situated at Grønlandsleiret 25, Munchies Falafel is known for its falafel wraps and Middle Eastern street food.

- Lorry Restaurant: Established in 1890, Lorry Restaurant is a historic venue that serves traditional Norwegian cuisine with a touch of modern influence. Located at Parkveien 12, 0350 Oslo, this iconic restaurant offers a warm and inviting ambiance. Some must-try dishes include rakfisk (fermented fish), (salted cod), and kjøttkaker (Norwegian meatballs).

- Olympen: Situated in the heart of Oslo's bustling city center at Grønland 15, 0188 Oslo, Olympen is a legendary restaurant with a history dating back to 1892. Known for its traditional Norwegian fare, Olympen boasts a charming interior and a varied menu. Don't miss their specialties such as fårikål (mutton stew) and lutefisk.

- Theatercaféen: Located near the National Theater at Stortingsgata 24-26, 0161 Oslo, Theatercaféen is a renowned culinary institution in Oslo. Established in 1900, this elegant restaurant combines classic Norwegian dishes with international influences. The menu includes delicacies such as smoked salmon, reindeer steak, and fish soup.

- Engebret Café: With a history stretching back to 1857, Engebret Café is Oslo's oldest existing restaurant. Nestled in the charming Kvadraturen neighborhood at Bankplassen 1, 0151 Oslo, this iconic eatery serves traditional Norwegian cuisine in a historic setting.

However, the restaurant's menu has evolved over the years and now includes a variety of international dishes, as well as Norwegian classics. Some of the dishes that are currently on the menu are; roasted cauliflower with pine nuts and chili, salmon tartare with avocado and dill, beef tenderloin with roasted potatoes and green beans, chocolate mousse with raspberry coulis, roasted cauliflower with pine nuts and chili, salmon tartare with avocado and dill, beef tenderloin with roasted potatoes and green beans, chocolate mousse with raspberry coulis.

- Lofoten Fiskerestaurant: If you're looking for a seafood-focused experience, head to Lofoten Fiskerestaurant located at Aker Brygge, Stranden 75, 0250 Oslo.. This restaurant captures the essence of Norway's coastal cuisine, serving fresh and flavorful seafood dishes. Try their signature dishes like bacalao (cod stew), king crab legs, and grilled salmon.

- Vippa (Address: Akershusstranda 25): Vippa is a food hall located by the waterfront and offers a variety of international cuisines such as Mexican, Italian, Vietnamese, Middle Eastern, and more.

- Smalhans (Address: Waldemar Thranes gate 10): Smalhans is a popular restaurant that serves Nordic-inspired cuisine with an international twist. Their menu changes frequently and features dishes from various countries.

- Hitchhiker (Address: Rosteds gate 15): Hitchhiker is a Korean fusion restaurant known for its innovative dishes. They combine Korean flavors with influences from other cuisines, resulting in a unique dining experience.

- Munchies (Address: Torggata 18): Munchies is a casual eatery specializing in American-style comfort food. They serve burgers, sandwiches, hot dogs, and other classic American dishes.

- Noodlepie (Address: Torggata 18): Noodlepie is a Vietnamese restaurant located inside the Mathallen food hall. They offer a range of delicious Vietnamese noodle soups, stir-fries, and other traditional dishes.

- Egon Restaurant (Address: Karl Johans gate 33): Egon is a chain of restaurants with several locations in Oslo. They serve a diverse menu with international options, including burgers, pizza, pasta, and salads.

- VILLA Paradiso (Address: Olaf Ryes 8): VILLA Paradiso is an Italian pizzeria that offers a wide selection of delicious pizzas made with high-quality ingredients. They also serve antipasti, salads, and other Italian specialties.

- Ekebergrestauranten: Situated at Kongsveien 15, 0193 Oslo, this restaurant focuses on Norwegian and European cuisine, emphasizing local ingredients and seasonal dishes. It offers stunning panoramic views of Oslo.

- Maaemo: Located at Schweigaards gate 15B, 0191 Oslo, Maaemo is a prestigious three-Michelin-star restaurant renowned for its innovative and modern Norwegian cuisine. They prioritize organic and locally sourced ingredients.

- Den Glade Gris: Found at Stortingsgata 22, 0161 Oslo, Den Glade Gris is a popular Danish restaurant in Oslo that specializes in serving traditional Danish dishes like smørrebrød (open-faced sandwiches) and Danish pastries.

- Ichiban Restaurant: Situated at Grensen 8, 0159 Oslo, Ichiban is a Japanese restaurant offering a wide range of authentic sushi, sashimi, tempura, and other traditional Japanese delicacies.

- Sawan: Located at Oscars gate 32, 0258 Oslo, Sawan is a renowned Thai restaurant known for its authentic and flavorful Thai cuisine. Their menu includes a variety of dishes like curries, stir-fries, and noodles.

- Oro Bar & Grill: Found at Dronningens Gate 19, 0154 Oslo, Oro Bar & Grill is a Brazilian restaurant offering traditional Brazilian dishes, including grilled meats, feijoada (black bean stew), and caipirinhas.

- Tatakii Asian (Grønland): Situated in the Grønland neighborhood, Tatakii Asian is a fusion restaurant combining Japanese, Thai, and Chinese cuisines. Their menu features sushi, sashimi, dim sum, noodles, and other Asian-inspired dishes.

- Istanbul Kebab & Pizza (Grønland): Located in Grønland, this restaurant specializes in Turkish cuisine, serving delicious kebabs, pita bread, falafel, and various types of Turkish pizza.

- Café Sara (Grünerløkka): Situated in the Grünerløkka district, Café Sara is a cozy café known for its Mediterranean and Middle Eastern dishes. They offer a range of options such as falafel, hummus, grilled meats, salads, and other Middle Eastern-inspired fare.

- Eataly (Stortingsgata): Eataly is an Italian marketplace and restaurant situated on Stortingsgata. It offers a wide selection of Italian products and dishes, including authentic pizzas, pasta dishes, antipasti, gelato, and other Italian delicacies.

- Dinner by Heston Blumenthal: Located at Tollbugata 31, this renowned restaurant serves modern British cuisine inspired by historical recipes. Dinner by Heston Blumenthal offers a unique dining experience with dishes like Meat Fruit and Tipsy Cake.

- Ling Ling: Found at Tjuvholmen Allé 14, Ling Ling is a contemporary Asian fusion restaurant combining elements of Chinese, Japanese, and Thai cuisines. They provide a vibrant atmosphere and a diverse menu featuring dishes like dim sum, sushi, and wok-fried specialties.

- Olivia: With several locations in Oslo, Olivia is an Italian restaurant chain serving classic Italian dishes including pizzas, pasta, antipasti, and desserts. Some branches are situated at Aker Brygge, Tjuvholmen, and Hegdehaugsveien.

- Sumo: Sumo is a sushi and Asian fusion restaurant chain with multiple locations in Oslo. They offer a wide range of sushi rolls, sashimi, tempura, and other Japanese-inspired dishes.

- Izakaya: Located at Dronningens gate 20, Izakaya is a Japanese restaurant specializing in various dishes inspired by traditional Japanese cuisine, such as sushi, sashimi, ramen, and yakitori.

- Noodlepie: Found at Mathallen food hall, Torggata 18, 0181 Oslo, Noodlepie is a Thai restaurant offering popular dishes like Pad Thai, Tom Yum Goong, Green Curry, Khao Soi, and Mango Sticky Rice.

- Dinner Restaurant: Situated at Stortingsgata 24, 0161 Oslo, Dinner Restaurant is an American-style eatery known for serving burgers, steaks, and other classic dishes

- La Perla: Situated in Grünerløkka, La Perla is an Italian restaurant that offers authentic Italian cuisine with a focus on traditional pasta dishes, pizzas, antipasti, and desserts like tiramisu.

- Beirut Restaurant: The restaurant is located at Youngstorget 2, Beirut Restaurant serves Lebanese cuisine, including dishes like hummus, falafel, kebabs, and grilled meats.

- Miss Sophie: Located at Torggata 32, 0183 Oslo, Miss Sophie is a French brasserie-style restaurant offering a range of French classics. Their menu includes dishes like steak frites, coq au vin, escargots, and various French desserts.

- Villa Paradiso: Situated at Olaf Ryes Plass 7, Villa Paradiso is an Italian restaurant known for its delicious pizzas and Italian dishes. They have a wood-fired oven and offer a wide variety of pizza toppings and flavors.

- Edo Sushi: Found at Skippergata 30, Edo Sushi is a Japanese restaurant specializing in sushi and other Japanese delicacies. They serve a variety of sushi rolls, sashimi, tempura, and udon noodles.

- Korea House: Located at Tordenskiolds Gate 14, Korea House is a Korean restaurant that offers traditional Korean dishes such as bulgogi, bibimbap, kimchi, and various Korean stews.

- Al-Amir restaurant: Situated at Storgata 28, Al-Amir is a Middle Eastern restaurant serving dishes from various Middle Eastern cuisines. They offer a wide range of mezze (appetizers), grilled meats, falafel, shawarma, and traditional Middle Eastern desserts.

- Vaca- Found at Tordenskiolds Gate 10, Vaca is a Spanish restaurant known for its tapas and grilled meat dishes. They serve a variety of Spanish tapas like patatas bravas, croquetas, and gambas al, as well as delicious grilled steaks and other meat cuts.

- Alex Sushi: Located at Slemdalsveien 70 B, 0373 Oslo, Alex Sushi is a popular Japanese restaurant in Oslo. They offer a wide range of sushi and sashimi options, as well as other Japanese delicacies like tempura, teriyaki, and ramen.
- Druen og Bønnen: Situated at Rosteds gate 13, 0178 Oslo, Druen og Bønnen is a cozy Mediterranean restaurant that serves dishes inspired by Greek, Turkish, and Middle Eastern cuisines. They have a selection of mezes, kebabs, falafel, and traditional Mediterranean desserts.

Restaurants that offer outdoor seating during the summer months:

1. Gamle Raadhus Restaurant
2. Olivia Aker Brygge
3. The Ekeberg restaurant
4. Restaurant Salome
5. Grefsenkollen restaurant
6. Olivia Hegdehaugsveien
7. South East Restaurant
8. Olivia Tjuvholmen
9. Sanguine Brasserie
10. Ling Ling Oslo
11. Aha
12. Lorry Restaurant
13. Tijuana

14. Sabi Sushi Vika terrace

15. Dapper Bistro

16. Bølgen & Moi Tjuvholmen

17. Centropa

18. Nedre Foss Gård

19. THIEF ROOF GRILL

20. Apostrophe

21. Shed 33

22. Engebret Café

23. FYR Bistronomy & Bar

24. Baltazar Ristorante & Enoteca

25. Eataly Ristorante

26. Bun's Burger Bar

Bakeries and Cafe in Oslo

- Tim Wendelboe: Known for its exceptional coffee, Tim Wendelboe is a renowned specialty coffee roastery and café located in Grünerløkka. They source high-quality beans and serve expertly brewed coffee.

- Åpent Bakeri: Translated as "Open Bakery," this cozy chain of bakeries has several locations in Oslo, including Grünerløkka. They serve freshly baked bread, pastries, sandwiches, and cakes. It's a great spot for a relaxed breakfast or lunch.

- Kaffebrenneriet: This Norwegian coffee chain has numerous branches across Oslo. They roast their own coffee beans and offer a wide range of coffee beverages. You can pair your drink with their delicious baked goods.

- Godt Brød: Another popular bakery in Oslo, Godt Brød, focuses on organic and locally sourced ingredients. They offer a variety of bread, pastries, and cakes. Their flagship store is located in Grünerløkka but they also have a location in Majorstuen.

- La Roche: Situated at Øvre Slottsgate 12, La Roche is a French restaurant known for its classic French cuisine, including escargots, bouillabaisse, and duck confit.

- Supreme Roastworks: Another popular coffee spot in Oslo, Supreme Roastworks is a specialty coffee shop known for its meticulous roasting process. They have a cozy atmosphere and serve a range of coffee beverages.

- Fuglen: Fuglen is a unique café that combines coffee, cocktails, and vintage design. They serve specialty coffee during the day and transform into a cozy bar in the evening. It's a great place to relax and enjoy a drink.

- United Bakeries: United Bakeries is a popular bakery chain in Oslo with several branches across the city. They offer a wide selection of freshly baked bread, pastries, cakes, and sandwiches. It's a convenient spot to grab a quick snack or breakfast.

- Pascal: Pascal is a renowned French bakery and café in Oslo. Their new location at Thorvald Meyers gate 19. They specialize in French pastries, bread, and desserts. The elegant ambiance and delicious treats make it a favorite spot for many locals..

- Åkebergveien Patisserie: located at Thorvald Meyers gate 30. Åkebergveien Patisserie is a delightful bakery serving a wide range of pastries, cakes, and sandwiches. They are particularly known for their French-inspired desserts.

- Kaffebrenneriet: A local coffee chain, Kaffebrenneriet focuses on serving freshly roasted coffee from various origins. They have numerous coffee shops across Oslo, where you can enjoy a cup of coffee and a selection of pastries.

- Fuglen: Fuglen is a unique café and cocktail bar that also houses a vintage design store. Located in Grünerløkka, it offers a retro atmosphere with a Scandinavian touch. They serve excellent coffee, homemade pastries, and light meals.

- Stockfleths: Stockfleths is one of the oldest coffee shop chains in Oslo, founded in 1895. They have several locations throughout the city, including Grensen 1 and Rosenkrantz Gate 11, each with its own unique charm. They focus on serving high-quality coffee and also offer a selection of snacks and pastries.

Suggestions for a night out:

Nedre Løkka Cocktailbar & Lounge

Location: Thorvald Meyers gate 89
0550 Oslo

Nedre Løkka Cocktailbar & Lounge is a well-liked cocktail bar situated in the lower Grünerløkka area of Oslo. The bar's design takes inspiration from the neighborhood's history and various cocktail bars in New York, creating a classic interior.

By blending Grünerløkka's culture and history with the vibrant cocktail scene of New York, they offer an impressive array of flavors and exciting cocktails. Their drinks are crafted using Norwegian ingredients but with an American twist, adding to their unique appeal.

Guests have the option to reserve a table in either the lounge or on the first floor, catering to those who prefer a more private setting. Moreover, Nedre Løkka provides a meeting room available for rent, making it possible to organize private or business events there.

Nedre Løkka Cocktailbar & Lounge takes pride in its commitment to environmental sustainability, as evidenced by its Eco-Lighthouse certification.

Underground Golf Club

Located at Industrigata 36 in Oslo, the Underground Golf Club is a delightful blend of pizza, refreshing drinks, and miniature golf. Drawing inspiration from the crazy golf concept, the golf course boasts 18 challenging and diverse holes.

For golfers and non-golfing friends alike, Barry's Pizza Shack prepares thin-crust pizzas with top-notch toppings. The club's bar offers a wide selection of drinks and cocktails, and there's a spacious backyard with a pergola to provide shelter from the elements.

At Underground Golf Club, you can not only enjoy a fun game of miniature golf but also host various events, parties, and even miniature golf tournaments. It's a perfect spot for both casual hangouts and special occasions.

Underground Golf Club takes pride in being Eco-Lighthouse certified, reflecting their dedication to environmental sustainability.

Torggata Botaniske

Location:

Torggata 17 B 0183 Oslo

The botanic cocktail bar is adorned with climbing plants and features its own greenhouse, offering drinks infused with fresh ingredients and botanic elements.

Reservations in advance are not available; they only accept walk-in customers.

Shufl

Location:

Holmens Gate 5 0250 Oslo jShufl, located at Holmens Gate 5, Oslo, offers a unique combination of gaming and dining experiences. This place, known for "Gastro Gaming," provides fantastic gaming experiences along with top-quality food and drinks. The venue is situated centrally on Aker Brygge, making it a great choice for gatherings with friends and colleagues.

The spacious and stylish premises at Shufl can accommodate larger events and parties, with the option to have private zones. They boast 12 high-tech shuffleboards with digital scoreboards and have a dedicated restaurant department that serves an 8-course Chef's Menu and à la carte dishes.

Whether you're planning an after-work party, summer celebration, gathering, bachelor party, or any other special event, Shufl can assist in creating a perfect evening for you and your friends. For bookings or more information, you can visit their website or send them an email.

Duckpin

Location:

Torggata 28 0183 Oslo Duckpin, located at Torggata 28 in Oslo, is Norway's only short lane bowling alley, conveniently situated in the city center. Unlike traditional bowling, Duckpin uses smaller balls, and there's no need for bowling shoes.

Apart from offering a unique bowling experience, Duckpin also serves delicious food. Being the first Duckpin restaurant in Europe, they offer a delightful combination of bowling and dining. The restaurant specializes in American fusion cuisine, including mouthwatering barbecue dishes cooked on a charcoal grill. They have a well-stocked bar with soft drinks and other beverages, as well as a dedicated lounge area for pinball, arcade games, and karaoke.

Duckpin frequently organizes fun events such as bowling championships and music bingo to keep the entertainment going. It's the perfect place to spend an enjoyable night with games and fun activities.

Market and street food

When it comes to food markets and street food in Oslo, there are several options worth exploring.

- Mathallen Oslo: Located in the Vulkan area of Oslo, Mathallen is a vibrant food hall showcasing a wide variety of local and international food. You can find fresh produce, artisanal products, and numerous eateries serving everything from sushi and pizza to Norwegian specialties. Address: Vulkan 5, 0178 Oslo.

- Vulkan Street Food: Situated in the same area as Mathallen, Vulkan Street Food offers a range of global street food options. The lively atmosphere, outdoor seating, and diverse cuisine make it a popular choice. Address: Vulkan 22, 0175 Oslo.

- Oslo Street Food: Nestled in the city center, Oslo Street Food is a food court featuring different food stalls serving international dishes. It's an excellent place to try out diverse flavors in a casual setting. Address: Torggata 16, 0181 Oslo.

- Mathallen Grünerløkka: This smaller version of Mathallen in Grünerløkka showcases local and international food specialties. It offers a cozy environment for enjoying a meal or exploring various food products. Address: Maridalsveien 17, 0175 Oslo.

- Aker Brygge: Aker Brygge is a waterfront area with numerous restaurants and cafes. While it's not a food market per se, you can find various dining options offering both Norwegian and international cuisine. It's a picturesque location to enjoy a meal by the sea. Address: Stranden 1, 0250 Oslo.

- Grønland Basar: Situated in the Grønland neighborhood. Grønland Basar is located at Tøyengata 2, 0667 Oslo. This multicultural market offers a blend of Middle Eastern, Asian, and African ingredients. You'll find colorful spice shops, halal butchers, and fresh produce stands, making it an ideal place to explore and sample exotic flavors.

- Smorgas Chef: Smørgas Chef Oslo is located at Rådhusgata 20, 0151 Oslo. For a taste of traditional Norwegian cuisine, visit Smorgas Chef at Tjuvholmen. This restaurant serves classic Norwegian dishes with a modern twist, such as gravlax (cured salmon), fish soup, and reindeer filet.

- Food Trucks: Keep an eye out for food trucks scattered across the city. They often appear at events, festivals, and popular spots like Youngstorget and Aker Brygge. These food trucks offer a range of cuisines, from burgers and hot dogs to gourmet grilled cheese sandwiches and Korean barbecue.

- Grunerløkka Lørdagsmarked: located at Abdis gate 2, 0556 Oslo, Norway. It is open every Saturday from 10am to 4pm. The Grunerløkka Lørdagsmarked, which is now open on both Saturdays and Sundays, is located in the trendy neighborhood of Grunerløkka in Oslo. This market offers organic produce, artisanal food products, local handicrafts, and street food options.

- Youngstorget Food Court: Youngstorget 1, 0181 Oslo, Norway. Youngstorget Food Court is a bustling market hall with a range of vendors serving international street food. You can enjoy flavors from countries like Thailand, Vietnam, Greece, and Italy, among others. The vibrant atmosphere and communal seating make it a popular spot for lunch or dinner.

- Barcode Street Food: Dronning Eufemias gate 14, 0191 Oslo. The food court is open from 11am to 1am every day of the week. It is renowned for its contemporary architecture and stylish restaurants, with a strong focus on promoting local and sustainable food choices.

- Torvehallene Oslo: This covered market features more than 30 stalls offering fresh produce, baked goods, prepared foods, and local goods. It's open year-round and provides a diverse selection of Norwegian specialties.

Oslo finest roof terraces

Oslo continues to expand, offering increasingly captivating views of the cityscape, there's no better way to appreciate it than from a rooftop bathed in the sun?

Oslo's finest rooftop restaurants:

1. The Top Bar: Savor cocktails while enjoying a scenic vista.

2. The Top Restaurant: Experience Nordic cuisine from the upper level.

3. Summit Bar: Located on the 21st floor of the Radisson Blu Scandinavia Hotel, this bar boasts unique cocktails and a stunning view of Oslo and the Oslofjord.

4. Eight Rooftop Bar: Delight in small dishes and refreshing Nordic beverages while taking in the panoramic view from the roof terrace of the Grand Hotel.

5. Ling Ling Oslo: Scandinavia's first Hakkasan restaurant, offering a delightful blend of food and drinks.

6. Sabi Sushi Vika terrace: An informal Japanese eatery in Vika with an izakaya concept, emphasizing both food and drink.

7. BA3: Frogner's all-in-one destination featuring a restaurant, cocktail bar, and nightclub.

8. Calmeyer's Garden: A cocktail club situated on the 13th floor of Clarion Hotel The Hub, providing a pleasant viewpoint of Oslo. The bar strives to...

9. Nodee Sky: Elegant surroundings accompany modern Japanese dishes, creating a unique ambiance on the 13th and 14th floors.

10. Thief roof grill: Indulge in delectable summer dishes while reveling in the unforgettable views at this grill restaurant.

11. Centropa: Located in the new Deichman Bjørvika, Centropa offers a relaxed cafe upstairs for a light meal and a chance to appreciate the surrounding panorama.

12. Mint Roof terrace: Dine outdoors on the roof of Sentralen and relish the experience.

13. Tack Oslo: Discover Nordic-Japanese fusion cuisine at the top of Sommerro.

14. Cool: Enjoy a rooftop terrace featuring barbecue, shuffleboard, and a bar.

15. City Roof: Situated atop the Folketeaterbygningen, this centrally located bar provides a roof terrace for relaxation.

16. BAR Volcano: Unwind on the roof terrace at Vulkan and soak in the atmosphere.

17. Bistro Tolvte & Kranen: Delight in a classic cocktail on the roof or savor a satisfying meal on the floor below.

18. S4 RoofTop: Experience a restaurant and bar on a rooftop terrace in the heart of Oslo.

These rooftop venues offer a range of options to suit various tastes and preferences, providing an opportunity to enjoy Oslo's charm from a different vantage point.

Attractions for children in Oslo include various museums where they can explore, play, and learn. Some notable ones are:

1. Holmenkollen National Facility: A modern facility for cross-country skiing, biathlon, and jumping.

2. Nobel Peace Center: A unique museum showcasing inspiring stories about the Nobel Peace Prize and peace efforts.

3. Norwegian Maritime Museum: An exciting museum set in a maritime environment, sharing captivating stories.

4. Bærum Works: A historic trading post with workshops, galleries, restaurants, and a child-friendly sculpture park.

5. Historical Museum: The largest collection of objects from prehistoric times and the Middle Ages in Norway.

6. Oslo Reptile Park: A place to meet live snakes, monkeys, crocodiles, turtles, and other fascinating creatures.

7. Viking Ship House (closed for renovations): An attraction featuring Viking ships (currently closed).

8. The Rose Castle: A magnificent art installation in Holmenkollen commemorating historical events.

9. Technical Museum: Norway's National Museum of Technology and Science, offering interactive learning experiences.

10. The National Museum: The Nordic region's largest art museum, showcasing both old and modern art.

11. Intercultural Museum: Sheds light on immigration history and cultural changes in Norwegian society.

12. Frammuseet: Visit the world's strongest wooden ship, Fram, which has ventured farthest north and south.

13. Norwegian Folkmuseum: Travel back in time at one of the world's largest open-air museums.

14. The Viking Planet: Norway's first digital Viking museum, offering a multisensory exploration of the Viking Age.

15. The Kon-Tiki Museum: Honoring Thor Heyerdahl's famous expedition across the Pacific on the raft Kon-Tiki.

16. Vigelandsparken: A sculpture park in Frognerparken, featuring over 200 sculptures by Gustav Vigeland.

17. MUNCH: Discover the artistry and life of Edvard Munch in an innovative exhibition.

18. Paradox Museum Oslo: An engaging museum that explores the concept of paradox in a fun and exciting way.

19. Stovner tower: Norway's longest tower, providing panoramic views of the surrounding area.

20. The Swedish Cancer Society's Science Centre: A museum highlighting important stories about public health.

21. Natural History Museum: Explore the diverse wonders of nature in the heart of the city.

22. Bygdøy: A peninsula housing several popular museums, making it a must-visit for museum enthusiasts.

23. The climate house: Experience interactive exhibits that depict a world affected by climate change.

24. The Long Islands: Langøyene offers various amenities, including a large bathing beach and naturist beach.

25. The fire museum in Oslo: Showcasing Oslo's rich fire history in a dedicated museum.

26. Deichman Bjørvika: Oslo's main library, providing books, activities, art, and film for all ages.

27. The pop center: A museum dedicated to popular music in Oslo.

28. Bogstad farm: Explore the beautiful Bogstad manor, once the home of notable figures.

29. The troll: Discover the Kollentrollet sculpture on Gratishaugen, overlooking the Holmenkollen ski jumping hill.

30. Parish water: An open space offering opportunities for outdoor activities like picnics, swimming, and fishing.

31. Technical Museum: The Technical Museum in Oslo is an interactive museum that showcases the wonders of science, technology, and industry. Children can engage in hands-on experiments, explore the principles of physics and mechanics, and learn about inventions and innovations that have shaped the world we live in. The museum offers a range of exhibits, workshops, and demonstrations.

32. TusenFryd: TusenFryd is the largest amusement park in Norway and offers a wide array of thrilling rides and attractions for children of all ages. From roller coasters and water rides to carousels and playgrounds, there's something for everyone. The park also hosts live shows, entertainment events, and various food options for a fun-filled day out with the family.

33. SNOW: SNOW is an indoor winter park located in Oslo where children can experience the excitement of skiing, snowboarding, and other winter activities all year round. It features different slopes

suitable for various skill levels, equipment rental, and professional instructors to guide beginners. SNOW also provides a cozy lounge area and restaurants for a complete winter sports experience.

34. EKT Riding School and Animal Park: EKT Riding School and Animal Park is a unique attraction where children can experience horse riding and interact with various farm animals. They offer riding lessons for children of all ages and skill levels, as well as opportunities to meet and feed friendly farm animals like goats, pigs, chickens, and rabbits.

35. Deichman Bjørvika: Deichmann Bjørvika is a modern public library in Oslo that offers a range of services and activities for children. It has a dedicated children's section with a vast collection of books, storytelling sessions, workshops, and creative spaces for kids to explore their imagination and love for reading.

36. The pop center: The pop center is a cultural hub in Oslo that focuses on music, art, and pop culture. It offers exhibitions, workshops, and interactive experiences that introduce children to different forms of creative expression. From music workshops and instrument demonstrations to art installations and digital media, the pop center provides a dynamic and engaging environment for children to immerse themselves in the world of pop culture.

Oslo cheap eat

Discover budget-friendly options in Oslo with dinner prices under 200 NOK, excluding alcoholic beverages due to Norway's excise taxes. For a more budget-friendly experience, explore the affordable choices on

Grønlandsleiret and Torggata streets, where you'll also find a variety of take-away options such as kebabs and burgers scattered throughout the city.

1. Kaffistova: Known for generous portions of homemade Norwegian specialties at reasonable prices.
2. Oslo Street Food: A food hall in the city center with various food stalls to choose from.
3. Haralds Vaffel: A waffle shop offering tasty waffles with a Swedish touch.
4. Tuk Tuk Thai: Central Thai restaurant decorated with bamboo from Thailand and a diverse menu of wok dishes, noodles, and curries.
5. Mamma Pizza Osteria: Casual eatery serving authentic Italian pizzas made with fresh, seasonal ingredients and imported hams and cheeses from Italy.
6. Krishnas Cuisine: Budget-friendly vegetarian restaurant at Majorstua with vegan and gluten-free options.
7. El Camino: A Mexican restaurant located at Frogner.
8. Ricksha Pakistani Street Food: Started as a food truck, offering tasty Pakistani food at festivals.
9. Dattera til Hagen: A colorful bar and café with a charming backyard.
10. Restaurant Schrøder: A classic pub and restaurant at St. Hanshaugen serving traditional Norwegian food in a relaxed atmosphere.
11. Syverkiosken: One of the last hotdog kiosks in Oslo, serving sausages prepared in the traditional way.
12. Istanbul Restaurant: Serves Turkish cuisine in a relaxed, family-friendly atmosphere with fresh and authentic ingredients.

13. Tullins Café: A casual café and bar near Holbergs plass with a diverse menu and reasonable prices.

14. Postkontoret: A bar and restaurant at Tøyen known for its really good Italian-style pizzas.

15. Munchies Grünerløkka: A popular place offering tasty burgers and sides at reasonable prices, with vegetarian and gluten-free alternatives.

16. Thai City Grüner: Simple restaurant offering good and affordable Thai food next to the Akerselva river.

17. Dovrehallen Bar & Restaurant: Informal place with a friendly atmosphere and traditional homemade Norwegian food at affordable prices.

18. Freddy Fuego Burrito Bar: Offers freshly made burritos with a variety of fillings.

19. Nam Fah: Serves authentic Thai cuisine prepared by experienced chefs using fresh ingredients.

20. Fly Chicken Steen & Strøm: Specializes in fried chicken with various sides.

21. Mediterranean Grill: A street food restaurant in Torggata street with shish, shawarma, and more.

22. Rice Bowl Thai Café: An informal restaurant near Karl Johan street offering Thai dishes.

23. Vippa Oslo: A vibrant food court with flavors from all over the world.

24. Café Sara: A cozy bar and restaurant in central Oslo with a large beer and food selection and a spacious backyard.

25. MelaCafé: Inspired by Palestinian, Lebanese, Turkish, and Syrian culinary traditions, the menu focuses on Mezah.

Child-friendly restaurants in Oslo that are perfect for families with kids.

These restaurants offer a variety of options, including indoor tropical storms, street food halls with play areas, healthy fast food alternatives, and delicious pizza and pasta.

1. Freddy Fuego Burrito Bar: Enjoy freshly made burritos with your choice of fillings. Nothing is frozen or fried here.

2. Villa Paradiso Majorstuen: This authentic Italian restaurant serves Neapolitan pizza and other Italian dishes cooked in a wood-fired oven.

3. Olivia Østbanehallen: Located in Østbanehallen by Oslo S, this Italian restaurant features a kitchen and interior inspired by Milan.

4. Pizza Crudo: Indulge in real Italian pizza made with high-quality ingredients and baked in a stone oven. The menu also includes antipasti.

5. Villa Paradiso Tivoli: Another branch of Villa Paradiso, serving authentic Neapolitan pizza and other Italian specialties.

6. Masala Politics: Experience the flavors of Masala cuisine at this restaurant.

7. Munchies Grünerløkka: A popular eatery offering tasty hamburgers and side dishes at affordable prices. They also have vegetarian and gluten-free options.

8. Olivia Aker Brygge: Enjoy Italian favorites in a beautiful setting with a view of the fjord.

9. The Ekeberg Restaurant: Located in a historic building, this gourmet restaurant offers magnificent views of the city and the fjord.

10. Le Benjamin Bar & Bistro: A cozy bistro serving authentic French cuisine and a wide selection of wines.

These are just a few of the child-friendly restaurants in Oslo. You can explore these options and choose the one that suits your family's preferences.

Chapter 10:

Shopping in Oslo

(Local recommendations)

Shopping in Karl Johans Gate

This is a popular shopping destination in Oslo, Norway. If you're planning to go shopping in Karl Johans Gate, here's what you can expect:

- Variety of Stores: Karl Johans Gate offers a mix of international brands, local boutiques, department stores, and souvenir shops. You'll find everything from fashion and accessories to electronics and home goods.

- Popular Department Stores: Two prominent department stores along Karl Johans Gate are Steen & Strøm and Eger. They offer a wide range of high-end brands, cosmetics, and luxury goods. You'll find popular brands like H&M, Zara, and Urban Outfitters, as well as Norwegian brands such as Dale of Norway and Moods of

- Local Designers: Oslo is known for its vibrant design scene, and you can find several shops featuring locally made products and designs. Look out for boutiques showcasing Norwegian fashion, jewelry, and home decor.

- Souvenirs: If you're looking for souvenirs or traditional Norwegian crafts, you'll find plenty of options along Karl Johans Gate. Look for shops selling items like knitwear, Sami handicrafts, wooden goods, and Viking-inspired souvenirs.

Opening hours can vary between different stores, but generally, shops are open from Monday to Friday, between 10 am and 6 pm, and on Saturdays from 10 am to 4 pm. Some shops may have extended hours on Thursdays until 7 or 8 pm.

Shopping in Aker Brygge:

Aker Brygge is a popular waterfront shopping and entertainment area. It offers a wide range of shops, boutiques, restaurants, and cafes. *Here are some recommendations for shopping in Aker Brygge:*

- House of Oslo: This iconic building houses several interior design and home decor stores. You can find a variety of furniture, lighting, textiles, and accessories here.

- Paleet: Located nearby, Paleet is a high-end shopping center that features luxury brands and designer boutiques. It offers a range of fashion, beauty, and lifestyle stores.

- EGER Karl Johan: Situated on the famous shopping street Karl Johans gate, EGER is a stylish department store known for its curated selection of fashion, beauty, and home products. It offers a blend of international and local brands.

- Filippa K: If you're looking for Scandinavian minimalist fashion, Filippa K is a great store to visit. They specialize in elegant and sustainable clothing for men and women.

- Moods of Norway: For a touch of Norwegian humor and fashion, Moods of Norway offers quirky and playful clothing and accessories. It's a fun store to explore.

- Design Forum: Located in the heart of Aker Brygge, Design Forum is a contemporary design store offering a wide range of Scandinavian design products. You can find furniture, home decor, kitchenware, and more.

- Byporten Shopping: If you're willing to venture a little further, Byporten Shopping is a large shopping center situated adjacent to Oslo Central Station. It has over 70 stores, including fashion, accessories, electronics, and beauty.

- Outdoor Gear: If you're an outdoor enthusiast, Aker Brygge has you covered. You'll find stores specializing in outdoor gear and equipment, including clothing, footwear, and accessories for activities like hiking, skiing, and fishing. These stores often stock top-quality Norwegian and international brands.

- Specialty Food Stores: Aker Brygge also offers a range of specialty food stores where you can find Norwegian delicacies, local cheeses, chocolates, and other gourmet products. These stores are perfect for picking up unique gifts or ingredients for a picnic by the waterfront.

- Souvenirs and Gifts: Aker Brygge has numerous souvenir shops where you can find traditional Norwegian souvenirs, such as Viking-themed items, trolls, reindeer products, and more. You'll also find shops selling handmade crafts and artwork, which make for memorable gifts.

- Waterfront Market: During the summer months, a waterfront market is set up at Aker Brygge. Here, you can browse through stalls selling local handicrafts, clothing, accessories, fresh produce, and much more. It's a great place to soak up the lively atmosphere and find unique items.

- After a day of shopping, you can relax and enjoy a meal at one of the many restaurants and cafes in Aker Brygge. The area offers a range of cuisine, from traditional Norwegian dishes to international flavors.

Shopping in Grünerløkka:

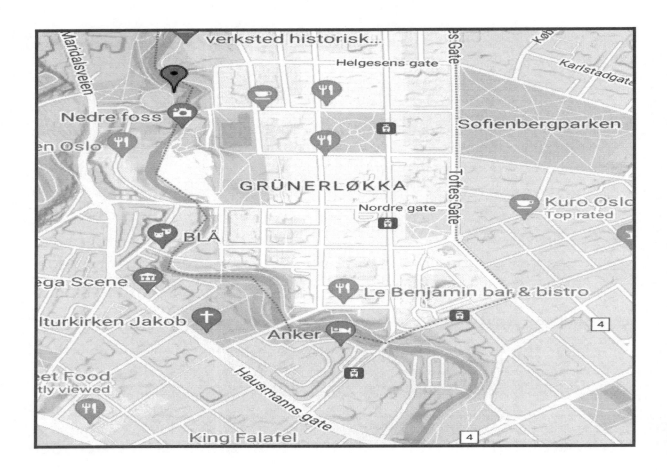

Grünerløkka is a vibrant and trendy district in Oslo, Norway, known for its eclectic mix of shops, boutiques, cafes, and restaurants. *Rcommendations for shopping in Grünerløkka:*

- Markveien: This is one of the main shopping streets in Grünerløkka, lined with independent boutiques, vintage stores, and concept shops. You'll find a range of fashion, accessories, home decor, and unique gifts.

- Grünerløkka Lufthavn: This popular concept store offers a curated selection of Scandinavian design, fashion, and lifestyle products. They have a wide range of items, including clothing, accessories, homeware, and even vinyl records.

- Fretex: If you're into thrift shopping, Fretex is a great place to explore. Fretex is operated by the Norwegian Salvation Army. It is known for its selection of vintage and retro items, including clothing, furniture, home decor, and accessories. They have multiple locations in Oslo, such as Grünerløkka, Majorstuen, and Ullevålsveien.

- Birkelunden Farmers' Market: If you happen to be in Grünerløkka on a Sunday, make sure to visit the Birkelunden Farmers' Market. Here, you'll find local vendors selling fresh produce, artisanal food products, crafts, and more.

- Vintage and Retro Shops: Grünerløkka is known for its vintage and retro stores. Some popular ones include Robot, Velouria Vintage, Frøken Dianas Salonger, and Fru Hagen Vintage & Retro. These stores offer a unique selection of clothing, accessories, and furniture from various eras.

- Design and Interior Shops: Grünerløkka is home to several design and interior shops where you can find Scandinavian-inspired home decor, furniture, and accessories. Stores like Pur Norsk, Klompelompe, and Habitat Oslo offer a wide range of stylish products for your living space.

- Grünerløkka Street Market: Located on Birkelunden Square, this street market offers a wide range of stalls selling vintage clothing, accessories, arts and crafts, antiques, and more. It's a great place to find unique and one-of-a-kind items.

- Mathallen Oslo: This indoor food market is a must-visit for food lovers. It takes place on weekdays from 10am to 8pm and on weekends from 10am to 6pm. Here you'll find a variety of specialty shops, cafes, and restaurants offering local and international delicacies. It's a great spot to indulge in Norwegian cuisine and pick up some gourmet ingredients.

- Independent Bookstores: If you're a bookworm, don't miss out on the independent bookstores in Grünerløkka. Head to Tronsmo Bokhandel, a renowned bookstore specializing in alternative literature and subcultures, or Outland Oslo, a shop dedicated to science fiction, fantasy, and comics.

- Designer Stores and Concept Shops: Grünerløkka also features several designer stores and concept shops. Visit URBAN, a boutique offering Scandinavian and international designer brands, or Pur Norsk, which showcases contemporary Norwegian fashion, jewelry, and home goods.

- Grünerløkka Lufthavn: This concept store is a mix of a cafe, bar, and shop, offering a unique shopping experience. You can browse through their selection of clothing, accessories, home decor, and other curated items while enjoying a cup of coffee or a drink.

Explore the surrounding streets as well, as Grünerløkka is known for its lively atmosphere and hidden gems.

Majorstuen

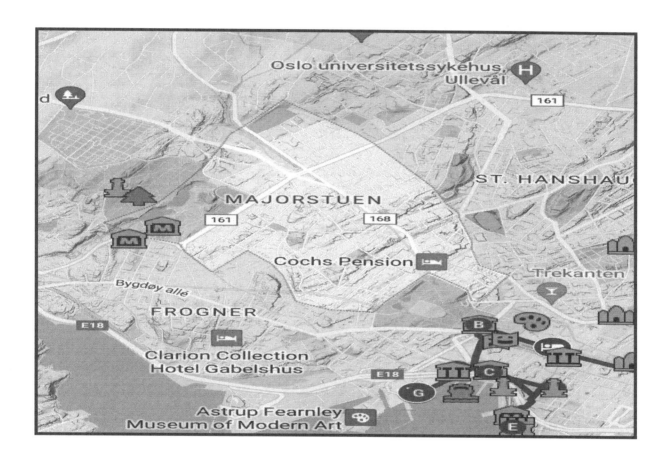

Majorstuen is a vibrant district located in Oslo, Norway. It is known for its mix of residential areas, green spaces, and a bustling shopping scene. Here are some popular shopping options in the Majorstuen district:

- Bogstadveien: This is the main shopping street in Majorstuen and one of the longest shopping streets in Norway. It offers a wide range of shops, boutiques, department stores, and popular international brands. You can find clothing, accessories, cosmetics, electronics, and much more along this street.

- Hegdehaugsveien: Another popular shopping street in Majorstuen, Hegdehaugsveien is known for its stylish boutiques, interior design shops, and specialty stores. It offers a more upscale shopping experience with a focus on fashion, design, and home decor.

- CC Vest: Located near Majorstuen, CC Vest is a large shopping center that houses over 100 shops, including fashion stores, supermarkets, home furnishing outlets, and electronics shops. It also has several dining options, making it a convenient one-stop shopping destination.

- Fru Hagen: If you're looking for unique and independent shops, head to Fru Hagen. It is a charming shopping street with boutique stores selling vintage clothing, handmade jewelry, antiques, and arts and crafts. Fru Hagen is known for its cozy atmosphere and eclectic mix of shops.

- Antique Shops: Majorstuen is home to several antique shops where you can find a variety of vintage items, furniture, artwork, and collectibles. These shops are perfect for those interested in unique and historical pieces.

- Fru Hagen: If you're looking for unique and independent shops, head to Fru Hagen. It is a charming shopping street with boutique stores selling vintage clothing, handmade jewelry, antiques, and arts and crafts. Fru Hagen is known for its cozy atmosphere and eclectic mix of shops.

- Majorstuen Farmers' Market: If you're looking for fresh produce, local food products, and unique handmade items, the Majorstuen Farmers' Market is worth a visit. It takes place on Sundays and provides a great opportunity to support local farmers and artisans.

- House of Oslo: Situated near the Frogner Park, House of Oslo is a shopping center dedicated to interior design and home furnishings. It showcases a wide range of furniture, home decor, kitchenware, and other household items from renowned Norwegian and international brands.

- Vintage and Secondhand Stores: Majorstuen has several vintage and secondhand stores that cater to those seeking unique and sustainable fashion items. Stores like Fretex, UFF Second Hand, and Velouria Vintage offer a diverse selection of pre-loved clothing, accessories, and more.

- Vestkanttorget Market: Held every Saturday, Vestkanttorget Market is a bustling outdoor market in Majorstuen. Here you'll find local farmers, food producers, artisans, and antique sellers.

It's a great spot to discover fresh produce, Norwegian delicacies, handmade crafts, and unique vintage treasures.

- Majorstuen Shopping Centre: This shopping center is conveniently located near the Majorstuen metro station. It houses several stores and services, including clothing shops, electronics stores, supermarkets, and eateries. It's a one-stop destination for everyday shopping needs.

Bogstadveien

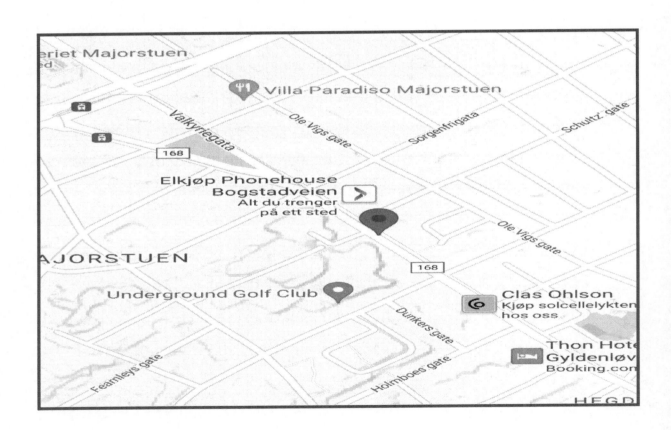

This is one of the most popular shopping streets in Oslo. It is located in the affluent neighborhood of Majorstuen and offers a wide range of shops, boutiques, and department stores. *If you're planning to go shopping in Bogstadveien, here are some things you can expect:*

- Fashion and Clothing: Bogstadveien is known for its numerous fashion stores and boutiques, offering both local and international brands. You'll find popular clothing chains like H&M, Zara, and Mango, as well as high-end designer stores.

- Department Stores: There are several department stores along Bogstadveien, including Eger Karl Johan and Steen & Strøm. These stores offer a variety of products ranging from clothing and accessories to beauty and home goods.

- Norwegian Design: Oslo is known for its design scene, and Bogstadveien is no exception. You'll find stores dedicated to showcasing Norwegian design and craftsmanship, offering unique items such as home decor, furniture, and clothing.

- Specialty Stores: Bogstadveien also houses various specialty stores catering to specific interests. These may include sports equipment stores, toy stores, electronics stores, bookshops, and more.

- Shopping Centers: In addition to the stores along the street, Bogstadveien is also home to shopping centers like Bogstadveien Galleriet and Paleet. These centers house a mix of shops, cafes, and restaurants, providing a more comprehensive shopping experience.

- Accessories: If you're in search of accessories to complement your outfit, Bogstadveien won't disappoint. You'll find stores specializing in jewelry, handbags, shoes, and other accessories. From trendy pieces to timeless classics, there's something for every style and budget.

- Weekend Markets: Occasionally, Bogstadveien hosts weekend markets where vendors set up stalls to sell handmade crafts, vintage items, food, and more. Keep an eye out for any events happening during your visit, as they can add an extra element of excitement to your shopping experience.

- Home Decor: Bogstadveien also features several home decor and interior design stores. Whether you're looking for furniture, decorative items, or home essentials, you can explore various shops offering a range of styles and designs. This is a great place to find unique items to enhance your living space.

Bogstadveien can get quite busy, especially during weekends and peak shopping hours. It's a good idea to plan your visit accordingly and be prepared for crowds.

Antique store and flea market

Here, you can find unique treasures, vintage items, and collectibles. Here are a few popular ones:

- Birkelunden Flea Market: Located in the Grünerløkka neighborhood, Birkelunden Flea Market is a lively outdoor market held every Sunday from spring to autumn. Here you can find a wide range of antiques, vintage clothing, furniture, vinyl records, books, and more.

- Fretex: Fretex is a secondhand shop operated by the Norwegian Salvation Army. It is known for its selection of vintage and retro items, including clothing, furniture, home decor, and accessories. They have multiple locations in Oslo, such as Grünerløkka, Majorstuen, and Ullevålsveien.

- Vestkanttorget Flea Market: This flea market takes place every Saturday in the Skøyen area of Oslo. It offers a variety of antiques, collectibles, vintage items, books, vinyl records, and more. The market is particularly popular among collectors and bargain hunters.

- Fransk Bazar: Located in the Frogner neighborhood, Fransk Bazar is an antique shop specializing in French and Scandinavian vintage furniture, home decor, and accessories. They have a wide range of unique items, including chandeliers, mirrors, paintings, and antique textiles.

- Retrolykke Vintage & Retro: Situated in the Grønland neighborhood, Retro Lykke is a vintage and retro shop that offers a diverse selection of clothing, accessories, home decor, and vinyl records. They have items from different eras, including the 1950s, 1960s, and 1970s.

- Fru Hagen Vintage & Antikk: Located in Grünerløkka, Fru Hagen offers a curated collection of vintage clothing, accessories, home decor, and furniture. The shop has a cozy atmosphere and is known for its high-quality items.

- Antikk Varehuset: Situated in the neighborhood of Tøyen, Antikk Varehuset is a large antique shop with an extensive collection of furniture, home decor, glassware, ceramics, and more. They specialize in Scandinavian and European antiques.

- Old Paris Antikk & Interiør: This antique shop in Frogner specializes in French and Scandinavian antiques. You can find a range of furniture, mirrors, chandeliers, and other decorative items.

- Vestkanttorvet Flea Market: Located in Majorstuen, Vestkanttorvet Flea Market is a popular outdoor market that operates on Saturdays. Here, you can find a mix of vintage items, antiques, second-hand goods, and more.

Strictly Norwegian design and souvenir

Oslo is known for its rich cultural heritage and design scene. When it comes to Norwegian design and souvenirs, you'll find plenty of options to explore in Oslo. Here are some places you can visit to discover Norwegian design and pick up souvenirs in Oslo:

1. Design and Craft Stores:

- Norway Designs: Located in the heart of Oslo, this store showcases a curated collection of Norwegian design, including furniture, home decor, textiles, and fashion.
- Dapper: A concept store that features a mix of Scandinavian design, fashion, and lifestyle products, with a focus on quality and craftsmanship.
- Fru Hagen: This boutique offers a range of unique Norwegian and Scandinavian design products, including jewelry, ceramics, glassware, and textiles.
- Heimen Husflid: This store specializes in traditional Norwegian crafts and handmade products. You can find items like woolen sweaters, knitted accessories, woodcarvings, and traditional folk costumes.
- House of Oslo: It is a design and interior shopping center with several stores under one roof. You'll find a range of Norwegian and Scandinavian design brands here, including furniture, lighting, textiles, and kitchenware.

2. Souvenir Shops:

- The Norwegian Folk Museum Shop: Situated in the Norwegian Museum of Cultural History, this shop offers a wide selection of traditional Norwegian crafts, including knitwear, woodwork, silver jewelry, and trolls.

- Husfliden: A renowned Norwegian craft organization with a store in Oslo, Husfliden sells traditional Norwegian textiles, such as wool sweaters, (traditional costumes), and woven products.

- Ting: With multiple locations in Oslo, Ting is a contemporary gift shop that offers a variety of Norwegian-designed souvenirs, home decor items, and accessories.

- Souvenir shops in popular tourist areas: Areas like Karl Johans Gate (the main street) and Aker Brygge (a waterfront area) have numerous souvenir shops where you can find typical Norwegian souvenirs like trolls, Viking-related items, knitwear, and postcards.

3. Markets and Fairs:

- Christmas Market at Spikersuppa: If you visit Oslo during the holiday season, the Christmas market at Spikersuppa is a must-visit. Here you can find traditional Norwegian Christmas decorations, crafts, and food.

- Designers' Saturday: This biennial event showcases the best of Norwegian design and craftsmanship, allowing visitors to explore showrooms and exhibitions by leading designers and manufacturers.

4. Galleries and Museums:

- The National Museum – Design and Decorative Arts: This museum exhibits a vast collection of Norwegian design, including furniture, textiles, ceramics, and glassware, spanning from historic to contemporary pieces.
- The Norwegian Folk Museum Gift Shop: Located in the Norwegian Folk Museum, the gift shop offers a wide range of traditional Norwegian souvenirs, handicrafts, books, and toys. You can explore items that represent Norway's cultural heritage.
- DogA (The Norwegian Centre for Design and Architecture): Besides hosting exhibitions and events, DogA features a design shop where you can purchase products from Norwegian designers.

Remember to look for the "Norwegian Made" or "Norsk Design" labels when shopping for authentic Norwegian designs and souvenirs. These labels ensure that the products are locally made and uphold the high standards of Norwegian craftsmanship

Chapter 11:

<u>Day Trips from Oslo</u>

Oslo Fjord Islands:

The Oslo Fjord Islands offer a beautiful and serene escape from the bustling city of Oslo, Norway. With their picturesque landscapes, charming villages, and a variety of outdoor activities, these islands are perfect for a day trip or even a longer getaway.

1. Getting There:

- By Ferry: Several ferry companies operate regular services to the islands from Oslo. The most popular departure points are Aker Brygge and Vippetangen.
- By Private Boat: If you have access to a boat, you can also explore the islands at your own pace. There are several marinas and docks where you can moor your boat.

2. Island Options:
- Hovedøya: This island is the closest to Oslo and is known for its beautiful beaches, walking trails, and historic ruins. Visit the Hovedøya Abbey, which dates back to the 12th century.

- Gressholmen: This island is a popular spot for picnics and barbecues. It has lush green meadows and scenic walking trails.
- Langøyene: If you're looking for a beach getaway, Langøyene is the perfect choice. It has sandy beaches, swimming areas, and facilities for volleyball and other beach sports.
- Nakholmen: This small island is great for nature lovers. Explore its forests, meadows, and rocky shores while enjoying peaceful surroundings.

3. Activities and Attractions:

- Hiking and Nature Walks: The islands offer numerous hiking trails that allow you to explore their natural beauty. Don't miss the coastal paths that provide stunning views of the fjord.
- Swimming and Beach Activities: During the summer months, the islands provide excellent opportunities for swimming, sunbathing, and water sports. Remember to bring your swimwear and towels.
- Picnicking and Barbecuing: Pack a picnic basket or use the designated barbecue spots on the islands to enjoy a delightful outdoor meal surrounded by nature.
- Kayaking and Canoeing: Rent a kayak or canoe and paddle around the fjord, exploring the islands from a different perspective.
- Cultural Sites: Visit historical landmarks such as the ruins of Hovedøya Abbey and explore the cultural heritage of the islands.

4. Practical Tips:

- Pack essentials like sunscreen, hats, and comfortable shoes for outdoor activities.
- Bring snacks, water, and a picnic lunch unless you plan to eat at the local restaurants on the islands.
- Check the ferry schedules in advance and plan your day accordingly to make the most of your time.
- Respect the natural environment and follow any rules or guidelines posted on the islands.
- If you're visiting during the off-peak season, be aware that some facilities, such as restaurants or visitor centers, may have limited operating hours or be closed.

Lillehammer

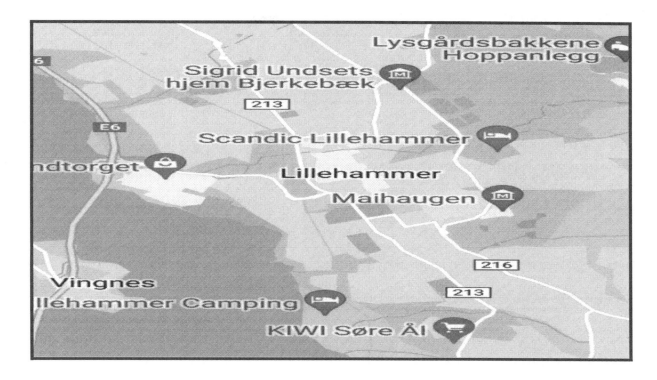

Lillehammer is a picturesque town located about 180 kilometers (112 miles) north of Oslo. Known for hosting the Winter Olympics in 1994, Lillehammer offers beautiful natural scenery, cultural attractions, and outdoor activities. To reach Lillehammer from Oslo, you can take a train or bus. The train journey takes approximately two hours, while the bus journey can take a bit longer. *Here are a few options for day trips from Oslo to Lillehammer:*

1. Maihaugen Open-Air Museum: This outdoor museum offers a fascinating glimpse into Norwegian history and culture. It features over 200 traditional buildings from different periods, including homes, farms, and stave churches. You can explore the exhibits, take guided tours, and participate in various activities.

2. Lillehammer Olympic Park: If you're interested in sports and winter activities, visiting the Lillehammer Olympic Park is a must. You can take a guided tour of the facilities, including the ski jump arena, and even try your hand at activities like biathlon shooting or skiing on the summer ski jump.

3. Lysgårdsbakkene Ski Jumping Arena: If you want to experience the thrill of ski jumping, head to the Lysgårdsbakkene Ski Jumping Arena. You can ride the chairlift to the top and enjoy panoramic views of Lillehammer. During the summer months, the arena is also open for activities like zip-lining and bobsledding.

4. Hunderfossen Family Park: Perfect for families, Hunderfossen Family Park is a fun-filled amusement park located near Lillehammer. It offers various rides, including a water park, a bobsled roller coaster, and a troll-themed area. The park also has a fairy tale castle and hosts evening performances during the summer.

5. Outdoor Activities: Lillehammer is surrounded by beautiful nature, making it a great destination for outdoor enthusiasts. You can go hiking in the nearby mountains, rent a kayak or canoe to explore the lakes, or even try your hand at fishing. Additionally, there are opportunities for cycling, horseback riding, and cross-country skiing, depending on the season.

The Telemark Canal

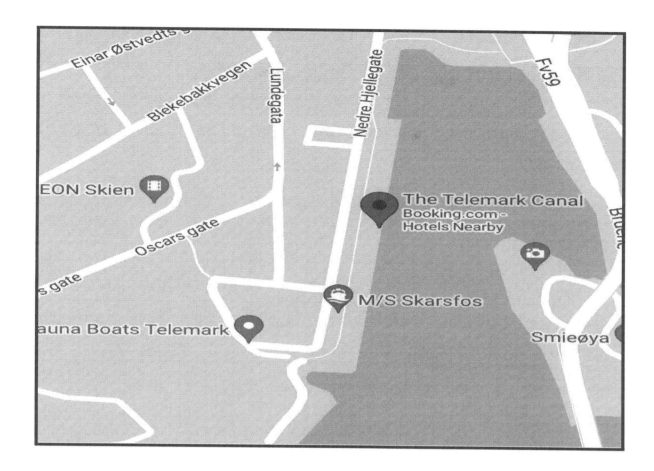

The Telemark Canal is actually located outside of Oslo, in the county of Telemark, Norway. However, it is possible to take a day trip from Oslo to explore this beautiful canal and its surroundings. Here's what you can expect on a day trip to the Telemark Canal:

1. Travel from Oslo: Start your day trip by taking a train or bus from Oslo to Skien, the largest city in Telemark. The journey takes around two to three hours, depending on the mode of transportation.

2. Skien: Upon arrival in Skien, you can explore the city for a short while before heading to the canal. Skien is known for its charming waterfront, historical buildings, and the childhood home of famous playwright Henrik Ibsen, which is now a museum.

3. Vrangfoss Locks: From Skien, continue your journey to the Voringfoss Locks, which is the highest lock system on the Telemark Canal. You can witness the impressive sight of boats being raised or lowered through the locks, creating a significant change in water levels.

4. Cruising the Canal: Next, take a scenic boat cruise along the Telemark Canal. The cruise will take you through several locks, picturesque landscapes, and small villages. You can enjoy the tranquility of the water, observe the surrounding nature, and learn about the history and engineering of the canal from the knowledgeable guides on board.

- Canal Cruises: One of the best ways to experience the canal is by taking a boat tour. Several operators offer guided cruises that take you through the locks, past charming villages, and along the scenic waterway. You can enjoy the tranquility of the canal while learning about its history and the surrounding area.
- Cycling: The canal also has a beautiful cycling path alongside it, which allows you to explore the area at your own Mappace. Rent a bicycle locally or bring your own and enjoy a leisurely ride while admiring the picturesque landscapes and stopping at charming towns along the way.
- Hiking: There are numerous hiking trails in the vicinity of the canal, providing opportunities for nature enthusiasts to explore the surrounding forests, lakes, and mountains. Some popular routes include the Lunde to Ulefoss hike or the Skotfoss to Løveid lock hike.

- Visit Historical Sites: Take the time to visit some of the historical sites near the canal, such as the historic Dalen Hotel, a magnificent Swiss-style hotel that dates back to 1894. Additionally, you can explore the Industrial Workers Museum at Vemork, which played a significant role during World War II
- Lunde and Ulefoss: The boat cruise usually stops at Lunde, a charming village along the canal, where you can disembark and explore the area. Lunde is known for its beautiful stave church and hiking trails. Afterward, the cruise continues to Ulefoss, where you can explore the historic Ulefoss Manor, visit the Ulefoss locks, and enjoy the scenic surroundings.

It's worth mentioning that the Telemark Canal is a popular tourist destination, especially during the summer months. Therefore, it's advisable to book your boat cruise tickets and plan your trip in advance to ensure availability and avoid disappointment.

Fredrikstad

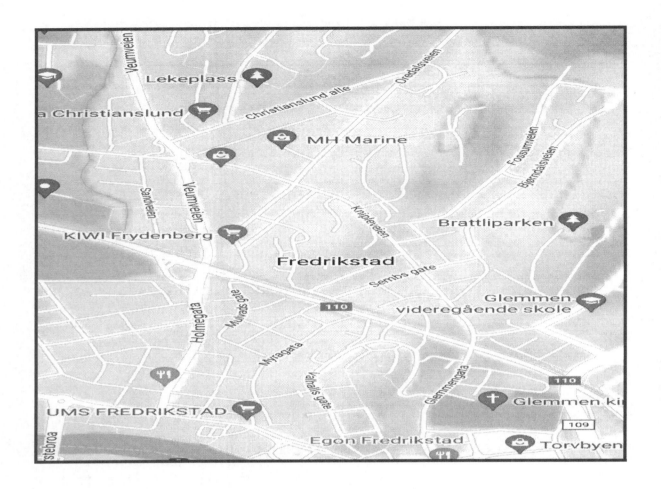

Fredrikstad is a charming city located in southeastern Norway, known for its well-preserved fortress and rich cultural heritage.

- Morning departure from Oslo: Start your day early to make the most of your time in Fredrikstad. You can take a train from Oslo Central Station to Fredrikstad, which is about a 1.5-hour journey.

- Explore Gamlebyen (Old Town): Upon arriving in Fredrikstad, head straight to Gamlebyen, the city's historic Old Town. This well-preserved fortress town is Europe's best-preserved fortified town, dating back to the 16th century. Take a leisurely stroll through its cobblestone streets, admire the old buildings, and visit the local shops and galleries.

- Fredrikstad Museum: Pay a visit to the Fredrikstad Museum, located in the heart of Gamlebyen. The museum showcases the city's history, from its founding to modern times. You can learn about the fortress, the local maritime heritage, and other important aspects of Fredrikstad's past.

- Ferry ride: Take a short ferry ride across the Glomma River to reach the other side of Fredrikstad. Enjoy the scenic views and the refreshing breeze during the crossing.

- The Waterfront and City Center: Once you arrive on the other side, explore Fredrikstad's modern city center and waterfront area. The waterfront promenade offers a pleasant atmosphere with cafes, restaurants, and shops. Enjoy a waterfront lunch at one of the local eateries, or grab a coffee and relax by the river.

- Visit the Fredrikstad Cathedral: Built in the 19th century, it is known for its impressive architecture and stained glass windows.

- Visit local attractions: Depending on your interests, you can explore other attractions in Fredrikstad, such as the lKongsten Fort or the Isegran Maritime Center. These sites offer further insights into the city's history and provide opportunities to learn about its maritime heritage.

- Kråkerøy: If you have extra time, consider taking a short trip to the nearby island of Kråkerøy. This picturesque island offers scenic nature walks, charming villages, and opportunities for outdoor activities.

Remember to check for any specific attractions or events happening in Fredrikstad during your visit, as this itinerary can be tailored based on your interests.

Halden

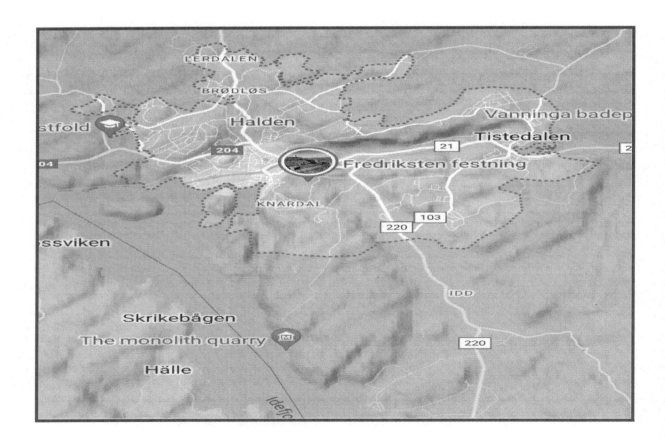

Halden is a charming town located in southeastern Norway, close to the Swedish border. Here are some suggestions for your day trip:

- Travel to Halden: Halden is approximately 120 kilometers (75 miles) southeast of Oslo. You can reach Halden by train or by car. The train journey takes around 1.5 to 2 hours, and the scenic route offers beautiful views of the Norwegian countryside.

- Halden Fortress (Fredriksten Fortress): Start your day trip by visiting Halden Fortress, a magnificent defensive structure that overlooks the town. The fortress has a rich history and offers stunning panoramic views of Halden and the surrounding area. You can take a guided tour to learn about the fortress's past and explore its various buildings and fortifications.

- Old Town (Gamlebyen): Take a stroll through Gamlebyen, Halden's old town. This well-preserved district features cobblestone streets, colorful wooden houses, and charming shops and cafes. You can explore the narrow alleys, visit local boutiques, and stop for a coffee or a traditional Norwegian meal.

- Immanuel Church: Immanuel Church is a beautiful neo-Gothic church located in Halden's city center. The church's architecture is worth admiring, and if you're interested, you can step inside to experience its serene atmosphere.

- Halden Canal: Take a leisurely walk along the Halden Canal, which runs through the town. The canal was built in the 19th century and connects the Halden River with the Tistedal River. It's a peaceful area, perfect for a relaxing stroll or a picnic by the water.

- The Norwegian Museum of Deaf History: The museum provides insight into the history and culture of the deaf community in Norway and showcases artifacts and exhibits related to sign language, education, and the achievements of deaf individuals.

- Tistedal Church: If you have extra time, you can visit Tistedal Church, located a short distance from Halden. This picturesque wooden church dates back to the 17th century and is known for its intricate woodwork and beautiful surroundings.

- Tista Nature Park: If you enjoy nature, head to Tista Nature Park. This park offers walking and biking trails along the Tista River, making it a lovely spot for a leisurely stroll or a picnic. The park is especially beautiful during the spring and summer months when flowers are in bloom.

- Halden City Museum: For those interested in history, the Halden City Museum (Halden Bymuseum) is worth a visit. Located in a charming old building, the museum exhibits artifacts and displays that tell the story of Holden's past.

Oscarsborg Fortress

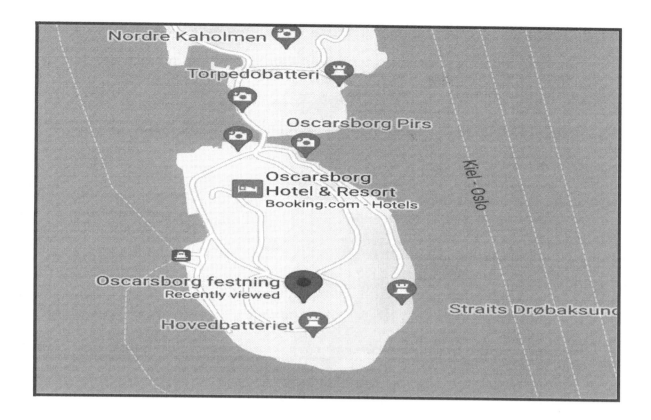

Oscarsborg Fortress is a popular day trip destination located near Oslo, Norway. It is situated on an island in the Oslo Fjord, about 50 kilometers south of Oslo. The fortress played a significant role in Norwegian military history, particularly during World War II.

To reach Oscarsborg Fortress from Oslo, you can take a combination of public transportation and a short ferry ride. Here's a step-by-step guide:

- Start by taking a train or bus from Oslo to Drøbak. Drøbak is a charming coastal town located near Oscarsborg Fortress.

- From Drøbak, you can catch a local ferry that operates between Drøbak and Oscarsborg. The ferry ride takes approximately 10-15 minutes and offers beautiful views of the Oslo Fjord.

- Once you arrive at Oscarsborg Fortress, you can explore the historic site at your own pace. The fortress is known for its well-preserved fortifications, underground tunnels, and military installations. It also offers scenic walking paths and viewpoints overlooking the fjord.

- Make sure to visit the main attractions of Oscarsborg, such as the Batteri 2 museum, which provides insights into the fortress's role in World War II. You can learn about the sinking of the German warship Blücher by the Norwegian coastal artillery, which was a decisive event during the German invasion of Norway in 1940.

- Oscarsborg also has a restaurant where you can enjoy a meal with a view of the fjord. It's a great spot to relax and soak in the historical atmosphere.

- Make sure to visit the main attractions of Oscarsborg, such as the Batteri 2 museum, which provides insights into the fortress's role in World War II. You can learn about the sinking of the German warship Blücher by the Norwegian coastal artillery, which was a decisive event during the German invasion of Norway in 1940.

- Oscarsborg also has a restaurant where you can enjoy a meal with a view of the fjord. It's a great spot to relax and soak in the historical atmosphere.

- After exploring the fortress and enjoying your time on the island, you can take the ferry back to Drøbak and then return to Oslo using the same mode of transportation you took earlier.

The Rock Carvings at Ekeberg

The Rock Carvings at Ekeberg in Oslo, Norway, is a fascinating historical and cultural site. Here's a travel guide to help you explore and learn about this unique attraction:

- Location: The Rock Carvings at Ekeberg are located on the eastern side of Oslo, near the neighborhood of Ekeberg. The carvings can be found in a wooded area on a hillside overlooking the city.

- History: The rock carvings are estimated to be around 5,000 years old, dating back to the Bronze Age. They depict various images, including people, animals, and symbols, providing insights into the prehistoric life and culture of the region.

- Visiting the Site: The site is easily accessible and open to the public. You can reach it by taking a short bus ride or a leisurely walk from the city center. The carvings are spread over a considerable area, so be prepared to do some walking on uneven terrain.

- Guided Tours: Consider joining a guided tour to enhance your experience. Knowledgeable guides can provide historical context, explain the significance of the carvings, and offer insights into the prehistoric societies that created them. Check with local tour operators or visitor centers in Oslo for available options.

- Interpretive Center: Adjacent to the rock carvings, there is an interpretive center that provides further information about the site and the people who lived in the area during ancient times. It offers exhibits, displays, and multimedia presentations to help visitors understand the significance and meaning of the carvings.

- Opening Hours and Fees: The rock carvings are open to the public year-round, and admission is free. However, the interpretive center may have specific opening hours and may charge a small entrance fee.

- Exploring the Area: After visiting the rock carvings, take some time to explore the surrounding area. Ekeberg Park is a beautiful park nearby, offering stunning views of Oslo and featuring numerous sculptures and installations by renowned artists. You can enjoy a leisurely stroll through the park's trails or have a picnic while admiring the scenery.

- Practical Tips: Remember to wear comfortable shoes and dress appropriately for the weather, as you'll be walking outdoors.

Bring water, snacks, and sunscreen, especially during the summer months. Respect the site by not touching or adding anything to the carvings, as they are fragile and protected.

- Visitor Center: Start your visit at the Ekebergparken Visitor Center, where you can gather information about the carvings and the park. The center provides maps, brochures, and audio guides to enhance your experience.

- Hiking Trails: Ekeberg Park offers several well-marked hiking trails that take you through the park's beautiful landscape and past the rock carvings. Follow the designated paths to discover different sections of the carvings and enjoy the serene atmosphere of the park.

- Interpretive Signage: Along the hiking trails, you'll find informative signs that provide explanations and interpretations of the rock carvings. Take your time to read these signs and gain a better understanding of the ancient art and its significance.

- Photography and Respect: While visiting the rock carvings, be respectful of the site and the surroundings. Avoid touching or damaging the carvings, as they are delicate and protected. Feel free to take photographs, but remember to follow any restrictions or guidelines provided by the park authorities.

- Other Attractions: Ekeberg Park is not only famous for its rock carvings but also for its impressive collection of modern and contemporary art. As you explore the park, you'll come across numerous sculptures and installations created by renowned artists.

- Facilities: Ekeberg Park offers various amenities to ensure a comfortable visit. You'll find restrooms, benches, picnic areas, and even a café where you can grab a snack or a cup of coffee.

Hidden backyard gems

Oslo offers a delightful city walking experience, but sometimes you need to take a break and recharge. Thankfully, the city is filled with hidden backyard restaurants that provide a cozy retreat for you to relax before your next adventure. Whether you're seeking a peaceful haven or a lively backyard party atmosphere, these hidden gems in the heart of Oslo will inspire you to explore and indulge in their unique offerings.

Some hidden backyard gems in Oslo that you should explore:

1. Prindsen Hage: Located at Storgata 36, Prindsen Hage is a charming garden fair nestled between old buildings in Brugata. With its enchanting atmosphere featuring strings of lights, pennants, long tables, and hammocks, it feels like a perpetual festival of good vibes. This 4,000 square meter backyard offers a delightful experience with flowers, food trucks, and uplifting music. You can enjoy refreshing drinks, exciting street food, play boules, walk barefoot on the grass,

and relax by the greenhouse. It's a magical garden that shouldn't be missed.

2. Angst Bar: Situated at Torggata 11, Angst Bar is a hidden urban treasure that can't be seen from the road. You'll need to go through the Strøget passage to discover this cozy and lively place. The bar is adorned with string lights, contemporary art, and green plants that create a colorful backyard oasis. The atmosphere is intimate and the music is just right. Angst Bar is known for radiating art, culture, and creativity, attracting a diverse crowd. On weekends, it turns into a vibrant backyard party where you can lose track of time.

3. Handshake: Located at Youngs gate 19, Handshake offers a living oasis tucked away behind tall buildings on Youngstorget. With carpets, big cushions, and a relaxed lounge atmosphere, this place is perfect for hanging out with friends. The backyard features large green plants, lanterns, and a cozy ambiance enhanced by pennants and strings of lights. You can enjoy refreshing drinks, small snacks, or indulge in a piece of cake while listening to funk, soul, and disco music. Handshake aims to provide a chill place where people can gather and enjoy each other's company, whether it's during the day or evening.

4. Stortorvets Gjæstgiveri: Situated at Grensen 1, Stortorvets Gjæstgiveri is a classic gem in the heart of Oslo. The beautiful, old building houses a cozy, yellow backyard with large tables and parasols equipped with heat lamps, ensuring a comfortable experience even in rainy weather. Dating back to the 18th century, the building itself adds

a historical charm to the ambiance. On sunny days, it's a popular spot, especially among tourists. You can enjoy coffee, beer, meals, and even jazz nights on Saturdays. It's a multi-use house that offers a delightful break from exploring the city.

5. Daughters of the Garden: Located at Grønland 10, Dattera til Hagen is a colorful and playful place that invites you to a backyard fiesta. Follow the lights through an art-filled corridor and enter a world filled with tall palm trees, colorful chairs, and vintage mopeds. The backyard radiates a playful and exotic atmosphere, nestled between old brick buildings. You can enjoy food, drinks, and happy music with friends while paying attention to the delightful details, such as the seating around a large tree. The backyard also features a DJ on weekends, adding to the lively ambiance.

6. The Asylum: Situated at Grønland 28, Cafe Asylet is located in one of Oslo's oldest wooden houses, originally dating back to the 1730s. This charming cafe offers a large backyard where time seems to have stood still. With long wooden tables, benches, and potted plants, it exudes a nostalgic atmosphere reminiscent of a bygone era. The menu includes traditional dishes, and you can enjoy soft drinks or draft beer. The backyard features a large tree adorned with string lights, creating a magical ambiance

Chapter 12:

<u>Events and Festivals</u>

Oslo jazz festival

The Oslo Jazz Festival is an annual music festival held in Oslo, Norway, dedicated to promoting jazz and related genres. It showcases a wide range of jazz styles, featuring both local and international artists. The festival has a rich history and attracts jazz enthusiasts from around the world.

The festival typically takes place over several days, with concerts and performances held at various venues throughout Oslo. These venues include renowned jazz clubs, concert halls, outdoor stages, and even unconventional locations such as parks and historic buildings. The festival program includes a diverse lineup of musicians, encompassing both established jazz artists and emerging talents.

In addition to concerts, the Oslo Jazz Festival often features workshops, seminars, and masterclasses, providing opportunities for aspiring musicians to learn from experienced professionals. These educational activities contribute to the festival's mission of promoting jazz and nurturing the local jazz scene.

The festival has gained a reputation for its commitment to artistic excellence and its ability to present a wide range of jazz styles, from traditional to contemporary, fusion, and experimental. It strives to create an inclusive and welcoming atmosphere, inviting both seasoned jazz enthusiasts and newcomers to explore and enjoy the genre. Oslo Jazz Festival can vary from year to year, including the lineup, venues, and dates.

Oslo opera festival

The Oslo Opera showcases a diverse range of opera performances, attracting both local and international talent. The festival aims to celebrate the art form of opera and provide a platform for artists to showcase their skills. During the festival, opera enthusiasts can enjoy a variety of performances, including classic operas, contemporary productions, and experimental works. The festival often features renowned opera companies, soloists, and orchestras from around the world.

In addition to the main performances, the Oslo Opera Festival may also include workshops, masterclasses, lectures, and other educational activities for opera enthusiasts of all ages. These activities provide opportunities for attendees to deepen their understanding and appreciation of opera.

The festival usually takes place in various venues throughout Oslo, including the Oslo Opera House, which is known for its striking architecture and world-class acoustics. The city itself offers a beautiful backdrop for the festival, with its scenic landscapes and rich cultural heritage.

Attending the Oslo Opera Festival can be a memorable experience for opera lovers, as it provides an opportunity to immerse oneself in the world of opera and enjoy performances by talented artists in a vibrant and culturally rich setting.

Oslo chamber music festival

The Oslo Chamber Music Festival is an annual event that takes place in Oslo, the capital city of Norway. The festival is dedicated to chamber music and showcases a wide range of performances by renowned international musicians, as well as emerging talents in the field of classical music.

The festival venue varies from year to year, but it typically features concerts in various iconic locations throughout Oslo. These include prestigious concert halls, such as the Oslo Concert Hall (Oslo Konserthus) and the University of Oslo's Aula Hall (Universitetets Aula), as well as other cultural venues and churches around the city.

The festival usually spans several days, with numerous concerts and events scheduled throughout its duration. It aims to provide a platform for chamber music enthusiasts to experience exceptional. During the festival, audiences can enjoy a diverse range of performances, including string quartets, piano trios, wind ensembles, and other chamber music formations. The festival often features both established and emerging artists, offering a platform for talented musicians to showcase their skills and interpretations of classical repertoire.

In addition to concerts, the Oslo Chamber Music Festival often includes masterclasses, workshops, and other educational events where aspiring musicians can learn from experienced performers. These events provide opportunities for young musicians to engage with established artists and gain valuable insights into the world of chamber music.

Oslo Pride

Oslo Pride is an annual festival and celebration of the LGBTQ+ community held in Oslo, Norway. It usually takes place in June and includes a series of events, such as parades, concerts, art exhibitions, parties, and educational seminars.

During Oslo Pride, the city comes alive with rainbow flags, vibrant costumes, and a festive atmosphere. The highlight of the festival is the Pride Parade, where thousands of people march through the streets of Oslo, demonstrating their support for LGBTQ+ rights and raising awareness about the challenges faced by the community. The parade typically attracts a large number of participants, including LGBTQ+ individuals, allies, organizations, politicians, and celebrities.

In addition to the parade, Oslo Pride features various cultural events and activities. These may include film screenings, panel discussions, workshops, theater performances, and concerts by renowned artists. The festival provides a space for dialogue, learning, and celebration, where people can come together to share their stories, exchange ideas, and foster a sense of community.

Oslo Marathon Festival

This is one of the largest and most prestigious marathons in the country. The festival typically takes place in late September or early October and attracts thousands of participants from around the world.

The Oslo Marathon offers several race distances to cater to different running abilities and goals. The main event is the full marathon, which covers a distance of 42.195 kilometers (26.2 miles) and takes participants on a scenic route through the city of Oslo. There is also a half marathon, a 10-kilometer race, and a fun run for children.

The marathon route in Oslo showcases the city's beautiful landmarks, including the Royal Palace, Oslo Opera House, and the waterfront area. Runners can expect a well-organized event with water stations, cheering spectators, and a festive atmosphere.

In addition to the main races, the Oslo Marathon Festival offers various activities and entertainment for participants and spectators. There may be live music, food vendors, and a race expo where participants can explore running-related products and services.

Christmas market and celebration

Oslo is known for its charming Christmas markets and festive celebrations.

1. Oslo Christmas Market (Julemarked): Located in the heart of Oslo, the Oslo Christmas Market is one of the most popular markets during the holiday season. It is typically set up in Spikersuppa, a park near the Royal Palace. The market features numerous stalls selling crafts, Christmas decorations, food, and drinks. You can find traditional Norwegian handicrafts, delicious Scandinavian treats, and hot mulled wine (gløgg) to keep you warm.

2. Christmas at the Folk Museum (Jul på Norsk Folkemuseum): The Norwegian Folk Museum hosts an enchanting Christmas celebration showcasing traditional Norwegian holiday customs and traditions. The open-air museum recreates a historic village with old-fashioned buildings, festive decorations, and various activities like horse-drawn sleigh rides, singing around the Christmas tree, and traditional food tastings.

3. Youngstorget Christmas Market (Julemarked på Youngstorget): Youngstorget Square often hosts a Christmas market where you can browse through stalls selling arts and crafts, local products, and seasonal delicacies. This market typically offers a cozy and lively atmosphere with entertainment, music, and activities for families.

4. Christmas Concerts: Oslo's numerous churches and concert halls often hold special Christmas concerts featuring choirs, orchestras, and solo performances. Venues like Oslo Concert Hall, Oslo Cathedral, and various churches throughout the city offer a wide range of classical, gospel, and traditional Christmas music performances.

5. Ice Skating: During the Christmas season, several outdoor ice rinks are set up in Oslo. Popular locations include Spikersuppa, Aker Brygge, and Frogner Stadium. Ice skating is a fun activity for both locals and visitors and adds to the festive atmosphere.

6. Christmas Market at Spikersuppa: Located in the heart of Oslo, Spikersuppa is transformed into a winter wonderland during the

Christmas season. The market features numerous stalls selling handicrafts, gifts, decorations, and delicious Norwegian food. You can also find rides for children and an ice skating rink, adding to the festive atmosphere.

4. Ice Skating at Spikersuppa: In addition to the Christmas market, Spikersuppa also offers an outdoor ice skating rink. Renting skates and gliding across the ice is a popular activity for both locals and visitors during the holiday season.

6. Festive Food and Drink: Oslo's restaurants and cafes embrace the Christmas spirit by serving traditional Norwegian Christmas dishes. Look out for treats like lutefisk, pinnekjøtt, and rakfisk, as well as festive desserts like krumkake and julekake. You can also warm up with a cup of gløgg, the Norwegian version of mulled wine.

Chapter 13:

<u>Local Tips on etiquette and custom</u>

When visiting Oslo, the capital city of Norway, it's helpful to be aware of the local etiquette and customs to ensure a pleasant and respectful experience. Some practical tips are:

1. Punctuality: Norwegians value punctuality, so make sure to arrive on time for meetings, appointments, and social gatherings. Being late without a valid reason is generally considered impolite.

2. Greetings: When meeting someone, it is customary to shake hands and make eye contact. Norwegians tend to have a reserved demeanor, but they are generally friendly and polite. Greetings: When meeting someone for the first time or in a formal setting, a firm handshake is a common greeting. Norwegians may also greet each other with a simple nod and "hei" (hello) or "god dag" (good day). It's customary to address people by their last names

3. Personal space: Norwegians appreciate their personal space and tend to stand at arm's length when conversing. Avoid standing too close or touching someone unless you have a close relationship.

4. Tipping: Tipping is not mandatory in Norway as service charges are usually included in the bill. However, it is common to round up the

amount or leave a small tip as a gesture of appreciation for good service.

5. Language: Norwegians generally speak English fluently, so communicating in English should not be an issue. However, learning a few basic Norwegian phrases, such as greetings, can be appreciated by locals.

6. Respect for nature: Norway is known for its stunning natural landscapes, and Norwegians have a deep respect for their environment. It's important to follow rules and regulations when visiting outdoor areas, such as national parks, and to leave no trace behind.

7. Dress code: Norwegians typically dress in a casual and practical manner. However, in formal settings or high-end restaurants, smart-casual attire is more appropriate.

8. Alcohol consumption: Alcohol Consumption: Norway has strict regulations on the sale and consumption of alcohol. The legal drinking age is 18 for low-alcohol beverages and 20 for stronger alcoholic drinks. Public intoxication is generally frowned upon.

9. Queuing: Norwegians value fairness and orderly conduct. When waiting in line, make sure to respect the queue and wait for your turn patiently.

10. Removing shoes: In some Norwegian households, it is customary to remove your shoes when entering someone's home. Pay attention to cues or ask if you are unsure.

11. Gift Giving: If invited to a Norwegian home, it's customary to bring a small gift for the host. Flowers, chocolates, or a bottle of wine are popular choices. Gifts are typically unwrapped upon arrival and received with a thank you.

12. Queuing and Line Etiquette: Norwegians value fairness and respect in queues. Always wait your turn and avoid cutting in line. Maintaining a reasonable distance from others is also appreciated.

13. Silence: Norwegians tend to appreciate silence and value personal space. In public places like public transportation or cafes, it's customary to keep noise levels low and avoid loud conversations or disturbances.

14. Outdoor Activities: Oslo is known for its beautiful nature and outdoor activities. When hiking or exploring the forests and parks, be mindful of the environment, follow designated trails, and avoid littering.

15. Recycling and sustainability: Norway is known for its commitment to recycling and sustainability. Make sure to separate your trash and use the designated recycling bins when available. Additionally, conserve energy and water when possible.

16. Cashless Society: Norway is largely a cashless society, and credit or debit cards are widely accepted. It's common to use electronic payment methods even for small purchases. Make sure to have a card or mobile payment option available.

17. Smoking: Norway has strict regulations on smoking in public areas. Smoking is generally not allowed indoors, in restaurants, cafes, or public transport. Look for designated smoking areas if you need to smoke

By showing respect, being polite, and observing local customs, you'll create a positive impression during your visit to Oslo.

Safety Tips

1. Be aware of your surroundings: Stay alert and aware of your surroundings, especially in crowded places or tourist areas. Keep an eye on your belongings, particularly in public transportation and popular tourist spots.

2. Use reliable transportation: Oslo has a well-developed public transportation system, including buses, trams, and the metro. Stick to official and licensed taxis or use trusted ride-sharing services.

3. Secure your belongings: Pickpocketing can occur in crowded areas, so keep your valuables secure. Use a money belt or keep your wallet and phone in a front pocket or a bag that can be securely closed.

4. Beware of scams: As with any tourist destination, there may be individuals trying to take advantage of visitors. Be cautious of unsolicited offers or approaches from strangers and avoid giving out personal information or engaging in suspicious transactions.

5. Respect local laws and customs: Familiarize yourself with local laws, regulations, and customs to avoid any inadvertent violations. This includes being mindful of the consumption of alcohol and tobacco in public places and respecting designated smoking areas.

6. Stay in well-lit and populated areas at night: While Oslo is generally considered safe, it is still advisable to stay in well-lit and populated areas, especially when exploring the city at night. Stick to main streets and avoid poorly lit or deserted areas.

7. Check for travel advisories: Before traveling to Oslo, check for any travel advisories or warnings issued by your home country's government. This can provide valuable information on the current safety situation in the city.

8. Dress appropriately for the weather: Oslo experiences varying weather conditions throughout the year. Dress appropriately and be prepared for changing weather, especially during the colder months.

Wear sturdy footwear to navigate potentially icy or snowy surfaces during winter.

9. Emergency contact information: Save important contact numbers, including the local emergency services, in your phone. In Norway, the emergency number is 112 for police, ambulance, and fire services.

10. Trust your instincts: Finally, trust your instincts. If something or someone makes you feel uncomfortable or uneasy, remove yourself from the situation and seek assistance if needed.

11. Stay informed about current events: Before your trip, check for any travel advisories or safety alerts issued by your country's embassy or consulate. Stay updated on any local events or demonstrations that may affect your safety

12. Follow local guidelines: If there is an emergency situation such as extreme weather conditions, follow the instructions provided by local authorities. They will provide guidance on how to stay safe and any necessary evacuation procedures.

13. Keep important documents safe: Make copies of your passport, identification documents, and other important documents. Store them securely in case of loss or theft. It's also a good idea to have digital copies saved in a secure cloud storage service.

14. Carry emergency contact information: Keep a list of emergency contact numbers, including your embassy or consulate, local police,

and your accommodation. This information should be easily accessible in case of an emergency.

15. Have travel insurance: Prior to your trip, ensure you have travel insurance that covers medical emergencies, trip cancellation, and personal belongings. Familiarize yourself with the policy coverage and keep the insurance details accessible.

16. Seek assistance from your embassy or consulate: If you encounter significant challenges or need urgent help, contact your embassy or consulate in Oslo. They can provide guidance, support, and consular services if required.

Remember, prevention is key to staying safe while traveling. Stay informed, and exercise caution to minimize potential risks. If you find yourself in an emergency situation while traveling, it's important to stay calm and take appropriate action. *Here are some emergency tips :*

Medical emergency

- Call the emergency services by dialing 113 for an ambulance.
- If possible, ask someone nearby for assistance or go to the nearest hospital.
- Make sure to have travel insurance that covers medical expenses and keep your policy details handy.

- If it is safe to do so, activate the nearest fire alarm.
- Exit the building immediately by following the emergency exit signs.
- Do not use elevators; use the stairs instead.
- Call the emergency services at 110 and provide them with the location of the fire.

Natural disasters

- Norway is not prone to frequent natural disasters. However, in case of severe weather conditions or other unforeseen events, follow local news and instructions provided by authorities.
- If you are near water and there is a risk of a tsunami, move to higher ground immediately.

Lost or stolen belongings

- Report any lost or stolen items to the nearest police station and obtain a copy of the report for insurance purposes.
- Contact your embassy or consulate for further assistance, especially if important travel documents like your passport were stolen.

References

- United States Department of State. (n.d.). "Travel Advisories."
- Google LLC. (n.d.). Google Maps.
- local interview with the author.
- Local photographers
- Canva.com
- Oslo Municipality. (n.d.). Oslo official website.

Did you Completely enjoy your Iceland travel guide?

Help others make the most of their trip by leaving a review

Taking a moment to share your experience not only requires a few seconds but also assists fellow travelers in selecting the perfect guide. Your valuable insights will aid them in crafting the perfect adventure, steering clear of tourist traps, and hitting all the must-see spots. Your review has the potential to significantly impact someone else's vacation.

Navigate to the orders section on your Amazon profile and provide feedback if this guide proved beneficial for your trip.

Printed in Great Britain
by Amazon

38865390R00159